T0353143

learn to live your
dream
& success
is guaranteed

This book is dedicated to everyone who seeks success, but most of all it's for Pauline, Hannah and Zachary, who make everything worthwhile.

learn to live your
dream
& success
is guaranteed

— ian bruce —

foulsham

LONDON • NEW YORK • TORONTO • SYDNEY

foulsham

The Publishing House, Bennetts Close, Cippenham,
Slough, Berkshire, SL1 5AP, England

ISBN 0-572-02705-2

Copyright © 2002 Ian Bruce

Cover photographs © Powerstock

Printed in Great Britain by Cox & Wyman Ltd, Reading, Berkshire

Contents

Introduction

Congratulations! By purchasing this book you have shown that you want to get more out of life, and this book will enable you to do just that. It doesn't matter if you are male or female, black or white, old or young, thin or fat, rich or penniless, self-employed or even unemployed – this book will explain how you can start living the life of your dreams. No matter what your current situation is, you **can** achieve personal success, and this book will explain how.

Achieving success in any area of life is far simpler than most people ever dare to imagine. You don't need to be any more intelligent or talented than the average person. You don't need any existing wealth or personal contacts. All you need is the natural potential you were born with and the information contained in this book.

Having said that, achieving success is not an automatic process. You cannot expect simply to read this book in one evening and then have your life magically transform itself into something exceptional. It doesn't work like that. In order to gain any benefit from the principles contained in this book, you need to apply them to your life. Don't just read how to become successful: take advantage of your new knowledge, by actually applying what you learn.

This book is divided into two sections. In the first I discuss the mechanics of how personal success is achieved and explain how you can apply a series of principles in order to achieve any goal you decide to set for yourself.

The second section then addresses seven specific goals.

- Financial success

- Physical health and fitness

- Success in your chosen career

- Fulfilling personal relationships

- Mastery of your emotions

- A healthy family life

- Spiritual fulfilment

I have devoted one chapter to each of these, showing you the actual steps you need to take and the habits you need to adopt in order to achieve them.

By reading this book you will discover a whole new life for yourself, a life in which you can succeed at whatever you choose, achieve your goals and become the kind of person you have always wanted to be. Not by hoping or dreaming or wishing, but simply by applying the proven principles the book describes. You can make it happen!

Part 1

THE SCIENCE OF PERSONAL SUCCESS

Taking Control

WHAT IS SUCCESS?

The best way to begin a discussion of personal success is by defining what the word 'success' actually means. Unfortunately, this isn't as easy as it sounds because there are almost as many definitions of success as there are people in the world.

To some, success means material abundance and financial independence. These individuals think in terms of owning a large country house, stocked with fine antiques and works of art. They might imagine having several sports cars, a luxury yacht and maybe even a private plane or helicopter. Success to these people suggests dining in the finest restaurants, having a wardrobe full of designer clothes and wearing expensive jewellery.

To others, success means something totally different, such as a state of peak health and physical fitness. These people therefore equate success with the idea of looking like Jean Claude Van Damme or Cindy Crawford.

Then there are those who think of success in terms of reaching the top of the career ladder, writing a novel and getting it published, having a fulfilling personal relationship or simple feeling 'at peace' with themselves and the world around them.

Whilst these are all fair definitions of what success may mean in specific cases to different people, they all have their flaws. Consider the millionaire who can't hold a relationship together for more than a few months. Or what about the person who enjoys strong, healthy relationships but is steadily getting deeper and deeper into debt? Or the musician who enjoys great fame but is addicted to cocaine?

Obviously, none of these people demonstrates genuine personal success, for although they all may have achieved something worthwhile in one or two areas of life, they have allowed other areas to get out of control.

True personal success is much more than the ability to achieve financial independence, career success, physical prowess or fulfilling relationships, even though it can encompass all of these things. For the purposes of this book, we will define the term as follows:

Personal success is the ability to get any desired result in life.

To me, this definition is incredibly exciting because it embraces an infinite number of possibilities. It describes personal success in terms of an ability rather than any specific achievement, and therefore suggests by implication that individuals who have this ability can achieve whatever they set their minds on. All they have to do is decide what they want and then set about making their goals a reality.

BELIEVING IN SUCCESS

We have defined what personal success means, but why do some people succeed in life whilst others don't? What is it that enables one person to achieve all of their goals and desires whilst the next struggles even with the normal day-to-day routine of living? How do an élite few seem to get everything they want out of life whilst the masses spend all their time merely 'jogging along'?

The answer is very simple. The vast majority of people don't genuinely believe that personal success can be achieved by all. Instead, they allow themselves to be limited by one or more false beliefs, which hold them back from reaching their true potential. Since these false beliefs, or myths, are so common, it is important that we expose them right now so that you are free to apply the principles that follow and achieve the personal success you deserve.

False belief 1: Success is down to luck

This is the most common false belief of all – that personal success is due to nothing more than luck, fate, fortune or even the astrological sign a person was born under. There are an astonishing number of people who believe that success and failure are random events over which we have little or no control. 'You just have to play the hand you're dealt,' we are told, as if we are nothing more than players in some kind of cosmic casino with either God or the Chaos Theory (depending on your point of view) as the dealer.

The most dangerous thing about this idea is that if you really believe it you won't even try to improve your lot in life. And why should you? If God or the universe has stacked the deck of life against you, who are you to argue?

The fact is that personal success has nothing to do with luck, chance, fate, destiny, divine providence or any other such thing. This can be proven in a very simple way. Anyone who applies the principles contained in this book will succeed. There are no exceptions. I don't care if you are a Leo or a Virgo, an orthodox Jew or an atheist. This material works for all who use it, thus exposing the popular 'success is down to luck' idea as the false belief it truly is.

False belief 2: You need to be super-intelligent or talented to succeed

Another commonly held belief is that success is due to incredible levels of intelligence or talent. Again, this is nonsense.

Consider this: if personal success was due to above-average intelligence, then why do many very intelligent people fail to achieve their goals? The national register of unemployed people includes plenty of intelligent men and women, many of whom have first-class degrees and diplomas. At the same time, many of the world's most successful people did poorly at school and some have no formal qualifications at all.

Talent is also largely irrelevant. There are masses of talented people in the world who don't achieve the success they desire. Yet there are also masses of people with no great talent, who achieve astonishing levels of success.

So forget the idea that achievement in life is dependent on how much intelligence or talent a person is born with. These are by no means prerequisites for success. If you can read and understand these words, then you have more than enough intelligence and talent to succeed on a massive scale.

False belief 3: Success comes from environment

A third major false belief is that personal success is dependent on the environment you were brought up in. This belief states that the place and conditions around you when you were young have a defining affect on whether or not you are able to achieve personal success later in life. At first, the idea sounds plausible, but when you look a little closer you will find that there are so many exceptions to this rule that they shatter it altogether.

Consider the American TV hostess, Oprah Winfrey. She was born into an extremely poor family in a poor neighbourhood, was constantly victimised by racists and, even worse, she was sexually abused as a child. Now if that early environment isn't a recipe for probable failure in adulthood – according to the false belief – then I don't know what is. But in fact Oprah overcame all the odds, achieved phenomenal personal success and is now a role model for millions.

Although obviously unique as an individual, Oprah is not a one-off as far as succeeding in spite of a negative early environment is concerned. Take a look at the biographies of celebrities such as Roseanne Barr and Michael Caine, and you will soon discover that many were raised in environments that were far from what most people would consider conducive to great personal success in later life.

On the other side of the coin, there are an equal number of cases of people who have had every advantage and privilege – ideal early environments, if you will – yet who have gone on to fail quite disastrously in adulthood. From these observations it quickly becomes clear that the environment an individual is born and raised in has no real determining effect on whether or not personal success can be achieved in adulthood.

False belief 4: It's who you know

This is one of the ideas that I personally used to believe before I eventually discovered the principles that drove me to write this book. I, like many millions of people, used to believe that achieving success depended on belonging to 'the right crowd' or on being friends with people 'on the inside'. I now know this is completely untrue.

Of course, to achieve some goals in life you do have to work and cooperate with other people, but merely having contacts is no more a **guarantee** of success than having above-average levels of talent or intelligence. There are many people who have achieved success without knowing anyone of influence. And by the same token, there are an equal number who have failed in life despite being surrounded by, and friends with, some of the richest, most influential people possible.

If you have ever thought that success is a matter of knowing the right people in the right places, then take heart – it's a false belief, that you can and should put to rest.

The myths I have mentioned so far are ones that most of society tends to share as a whole. But there are other myths that we hold as individuals. We tell ourselves that we can't succeed because we're too old, too young, too thin, too fat, too plain, too attractive, too bald, and so on.

I know a man who sincerely believes he can never succeed in life because he is too short! And when I point out that many short people have had massive success (look at Napoleon, Danny DeVito, Tom Cruise, Olga Korbut) he defends his stance by airing another false belief, maintaining that those people have 'just been lucky'.

BEING RESPONSIBLE FOR YOURSELF

Why do we, both as a society and as individuals, insist on holding ourselves back by believing all of these false ideas? The reason is quite simple. **The majority of people simply don't want to take responsibility for their own success or failure.** The notion that we are all individually responsible for how successful we become is just too much to deal with.

Holding on to false beliefs is therefore our way of passing the buck on to something or someone else. We can't succeed because we aren't lucky enough, God doesn't love us enough, we aren't talented or clever enough, we don't know the right people, we don't live in the right town or country, we don't look the part... The list goes on and on.

Paradoxically, it is this constant barrage of false beliefs and excuses, together with a failure to accept total responsibility for our own lives, that prevents the majority of people from succeeding. If people put all their false beliefs aside and accept that they alone are responsible for their own personal success or failure, then achieving that success suddenly becomes a whole lot easier.

THE TRUTH ABOUT PERSONAL SUCCESS

Having dispelled the major false beliefs that many people hold concerning personal success, what is the truth? There are in fact several truths, and by the time you have applied the principles presented in this book you will have proven each and every one of them to yourself.

Truth 1: Personal success is available to all

The first truth is that personal success is available to anyone who genuinely wants it. You may think it ridiculous that someone might not really want to succeed, but in fact a genuine desire to improve one's life is not as common as you might think.

Human beings very quickly adapt to being unsuccessful. Having tried several times to succeed and failed just as many times, most people cope with their disappointment by lowering their expectations and settling into a dull but predictable routine. People tend to get a lot of comfort from this predictability. After all, if you don't aspire to anything of consequence, you are never disappointed. Eventually this apathetic attitude towards life makes seeking success seem like an uncomfortable, and perhaps even dangerous, idea.

This being the case, although personal success is freely available to all regardless of age, sex, colour, creed or any other variable, only a very few are actually willing to risk leaving their comfort zones behind in order to step forward and claim it.

Truth 2: Personal success isn't complicated

Achieving success in life isn't a complicated matter. In fact, it's downright simple, since (as you will soon discover) achievement in any endeavour can be reduced to a straightforward, never-fail formula.

Having said that, don't make the mistake of confusing the word 'simple' with the word 'easy'. The bottom line is that achieving success is not usually easy. It normally requires a lot of commitment, effort and plain hard work.

If I have just burst your bubble, then I apologise, but my aim in this book is not to make you feel warm and fuzzy, but to help you achieve tangible, real-world results.

The good news is that if you are working towards a goal that you have a burning desire to achieve, working towards it can be almost as exhilarating as achieving it. Indeed, sometimes the journey is more enjoyable than the destination. This is why so many people who have already achieved success in life strive to achieve even bigger and better things. Not because they are greedy or have huge egos, but simply because the journey towards new goals and objectives can be a thrilling experience in itself.

Truth 3: Personal success takes time

For some reason, most people seem to think that achieving success is something that happens overnight. It isn't. Achieving any worthwhile goal takes time and this could be days, weeks, months or maybe even years, depending on the specific goal you are working towards.

I once had a friend who was a stock market investor. He lost more often than he gained as a matter of course and a colleague offered to help him apply certain principles so that he could achieve his goal of becoming a millionaire. His colleague spent several weeks researching my friend's usual investment strategies and then devised an alternative that would be more successful. He explained that if my friend adopted the alternative strategy he could start with a £5,000 fund and, through a series of regular compounded investments, generate the required £1 million in less than six years.

As soon as my friend heard this, his jaw dropped. 'Six years? How could you possibly expect me to wait that long?'

And this from a man who had been routinely losing money for over a decade.

This little story highlights two points: achieving any worthwhile goal takes time, and unless you actually start you will never get to live the kind of life you have always wanted. Although we live in a society where we champion speed over substance (think fast food, instant coffee, microwaved meals and so on), when it comes to achieving personal success there is no quick fix.

The principles in this book will enable you to start moving towards any goal you aspire to, both swiftly and effectively. If a goal can be achieved quickly, rest assured that you will achieve it quickly. However, don't think for a minute that all results will come immediately because they won't. Personal success takes time.

DEVELOPING A POSITIVE ATTITUDE

Having established what is and isn't true about personal success, it is time for you to take your first step towards the life of your dreams. To do this, you must learn to develop a positive mental attitude.

We have all heard that positive thinking works miracles, and although that statement may be something of an exaggeration, it is true to say that positive thinking does go a long way towards helping you change your life for the better. If you think in a positive way, then you automatically begin to act in a more positive way, and the results you get in life are therefore more likely to be positive ones.

Unfortunately, developing a positive mental attitude isn't something that can be achieved in an instant. Your thoughts are usually habitual, and habits take time to change. However, you can make an immediate start in learning to think in a more positive manner by applying the following principles.

Adopt a positive life metaphor

We all have different metaphors to encapsulate how we perceive life to be. Some people describe life as being a test or trial. Others view it as a grind or, even worse, as a bitch. Whilst we are all free to hold our own opinions, none of these particular metaphors strike me as being tremendously empowering, and if you believe that life is a test, trial, grind or bitch, then in truth that is what you will perceive it to be in your own experience.

By adopting a more positive life metaphor, you can immediately improve the way you perceive your life. View your life as a game and any problems your encounter will be perceived as challenges that you can overcome. Regard your life as a dream and you will find it easier to detach yourself from any negative emotions you might otherwise experience. Think of life as a party and you will actually increase the amount of fun you get from each day.

Changing the metaphor you use to describe your life won't magically change what actually happens to you, but it will transform the way you perceive your daily experiences. So set yourself up for success **now** by adopting a positive life metaphor. Select one from the list below or invent your own, and note the immediate positive impact it has on your day-to-day life.

Life is:

- A game

- A dream

- A ride

- A gift

- A stage

- A party

- A movie

- An adventure

Seek out the positive

We all know people who go through life looking for the negative side. These are the people who focus hard on finding reasons why nothing will work and why things will always go wrong instead. Tell them about your hard-earned promotion and they will tell you how tough it is to have so much responsibility. Tell them how much money you've saved and they'll point out that it won't buy you happiness. Tell them that you've met the love of your life and they'll tell you it won't last.

The people who achieve and enjoy true personal success in life don't do this. Instead they seek out the positive side of life as a matter of habit. When facing a problem they ask themselves, 'How can I get something good from this?' or 'What can I learn from this experience?' They view the proverbial glass as half-full instead of half-empty. They take their eyes off the mass of any cloud and look instead for the silver lining that they know is always there.

Seeking out the positive side of life in this way might feel a little awkward at first – especially if you are used to focusing on the negative. However, if you practise this principle each day, then in a matter of weeks it will become second nature and you will wonder how you ever managed to live without it.

Talk yourself up

The third thing you can do to develop the necessary positive mental attitude is 'talk yourself up' with positive affirmations. All too often our internal dialogue expresses a constant stream of self-doubts, false limitations and negative commentaries, which can all prevent us from achieving our true potential. Positive affirmations, when used regularly, allow us gradually to 'reprogramme' this internal chatter so that it begins to encourage and support our efforts instead of trying to sabotage them.

The best way to use affirmations is to start by sitting down and identifying any negative or disempowering self-talk that runs through your mind on a regular basis. Here are a few very common negative affirmations that you might look out for, but bear in mind that this list is by no means exhaustive, so add any others that you know apply to you:

- I am too old/young/thin/fat/tall/short.

- Life is hard.

- Change is difficult.

- I am stupid/ugly/incapable/slow.

- No one likes me.

- Most problems are insurmountable.

- I can't!

- I am a bad student/wife/husband/lover/businessman.

When you are convinced that you have identified all the disempowering beliefs you currently hold about yourself and the world, replace them with new empowering affirmations, such as:

- I am growing as a person.

- Life is a breeze.

- Change is easy if I am committed to changing.

- I am intelligent/industrious/creative.

- Everyone likes me.

- Problems are opportunities in disguise.

- Life is an adventure and a game.

- I am a great student/wife/husband/lover/businessman.

Write your new positive affirmations down on a few index cards that you can carry around in your pocket and read them aloud to yourself three times each day. If possible, stand in front of a mirror to do this and speak each affirmation with as much conviction as you can muster. You might feel a little embarrassed doing this at first, but after a week or two it will become more natural, and after 21 days or so you will find that your mental attitude has improved quite noticeably.

Expect success

A final tip for developing a strong positive mental attitude is to **expect** success. Each morning when you get out of bed, tell yourself that something good is going to happen during the day, then continue with your normal routine with an expectant attitude.

This technique is incredibly simple, but very powerful. As you go through each day expecting success to show up, you will begin to think, speak and act a little differently. The changes in your attitude will be subtle at first, but before long you will find that you have actually become one of those positive, optimistic people who tend to do so well in life. Even better, you will find that the more you expect success, the more it tends to show up. I can't pretend to know how or why this happens, but it does, so start expecting success from this moment on.

By applying the four principles I have just described, you will automatically begin to create a positive mental attitude for yourself. Whilst a positive attitude alone won't make all your dreams come true, it will serve as a strong foundation on which you can build the kind of life you have always wanted to have.

Designing Your Destiny

*I*n the 1950s, a study was set up in the United States of America that tried to determine the difference between people who succeed and people who don't. A large sample of university students were questioned about their goals and dreams for the future, and then 20 years later these same students were questioned about their achievements or lack of them. When the second set of answers were compared with the first, something remarkable became crystal clear: success is enjoyed most easily by those who set themselves clear targets.

It was found that only three per cent of the original sample had set themselves written goals, defining what they would like to achieve in the future. When the sample group was revisited 20 years later, the three per cent who had set goals and written them down had achieved far more financial success than anyone else in the group. What is more, the three per cent were worth more, financially speaking, than all of the remaining ninety-seven per cent combined!

Of course, as we have already seen, financial success doesn't mean that this three per cent were necessarily any more fulfilled in other areas of their lives, but as a measure it certainly illustrates the importance of having clear, well-defined goals.

All too often people complain about the fact that they are 'going nowhere' in life. Yet if you ask them where in particular they **want** to go, the majority will respond with nothing more than a blank stare, because they just haven't got a clue. Some will respond that they want 'more money' or 'a better job' or 'better relationships' but these things aren't specific goals. They are vague wishes.

If you want to achieve goals, you first have to set them. By defining exactly what you want to get out of life and setting these specific goals down on paper, you will automatically place yourself in the top three per cent of achievers in the world. Why? Because the ratio discovered in that study in America has since been established globally: only three per cent of the entire world population ever bother to set themselves written goals. And guess what? This three per cent of the population is also the most successful sector of the human population!

Of course, there are hundreds of books currently available that tell you all about setting goals, but most of the methods these books teach are ineffective. You see, ever since that original study in the 1950s, many people who discovered the art of goal-setting assumed that more is better: they thought that the more goals you set for yourself, the more you'll end up achieving in life. Right? Wrong.

The more goals you set, the less focused you will be when it comes to achieving them. If you set just a few goals, then you are able to give these everything you've got in terms of time, energy and commitment. This ensures that the few goals are achieved in the fastest possible time. If, on the other hand, you set, say, ten completely different goals, it is unlikely that you will actually achieve any of them, simply because it is impossible to spread yourself in so many different directions at once and still be effective.

DEFINING YOUR GOALS

Now that you can see the importance of having clearly defined goals, it's time for you to create a blueprint of all that you would like to achieve and experience in the future.

Before you do that however, you should first understand a few basic rules that are essential to proper goal-setting.

Write down your goals

Every single one of your goals must be written down on paper – now. It is no good reading this chapter with the idea that you will return to it and put your goals in writing at a later date. You must write your goals on paper and you must do so immediately. The principles that are presented in the following chapters assume that you have all your goals already recorded in writing, so failing to follow this basic instruction will seriously hinder later progress.

Your goals should be written down in two stages. The first stage involves brainstorming, so have some notepaper and a pencil handy to make rough notes. When you get to the second stage you will take those notes and use them to create a blueprint of your future. You will need a separate notebook or pad for this purpose.

Writing your goals down on paper will help you to make sure that they are all as detailed and precise as possible. Imagine that you want a magnificent home built for yourself. Would you go to a developer and say, 'I want you to build the house of my dreams,' without first having defined in your own mind exactly what you mean? Of course not. You would spend a great deal of time and effort in getting the details of your dream home down on paper so that the developer can give you exactly what you have in mind. The same principle applies here. Writing your goals down ensures that you will later achieve exactly the goals that you first imagined.

Set specific goals

When designing your destiny, you must be as specific as possible. Don't just write, 'I want more money.' Instead, specify exactly **how much** more money you want in your life. After all, there's quite a difference between wanting £5,000 and £500,000. Similarly, don't write, 'I want to lose weight.' Instead, define exactly **how much** weight you want to lose – is it 2 or 22 kg (5 or 50 lb)?

To help you be as specific as possible, obtain brochures and magazines that detail some of the things you would like to have or achieve. If you want a new car, then go and buy a car magazine and select the exact make and model you want. If you want to travel the world, then obtain some travel brochures and decide not only exactly which countries you want to visit but also which regions you specifically want to visit in those countries.

Remember, the goals you set as you work through this chapter are the goals **you will achieve** if you apply what you learn from the rest of this book, so there is no room for fuzzy thinking. You must be specific.

Be honest

The destiny you will be designing through goal-setting will be **your** destiny, so don't make the mistake of designing something for the sake of other people. If **you** would like to live in a nice little village in Sussex, then that's great, but don't set it as a goal just because you think that it would please your parents!

Many people have become accustomed to living their lives in order to please other people. You must not allow yourself to fall into that trap. We all have our own lives to live, so don't waste yours by trying to accommodate everyone around you. If the people around you won't like your plans, then either keep quiet about them or buy them a copy of this book so that they can start taking control of their own lives instead of trying to control yours.

Be honest with yourself and with what you want out of your life. We are, after all, talking about **your** life, so don't waste it by designing something that pleases other people but bores the pants off you.

Aim high

As you set your goals, remember that there are no limitations other than those you impose upon yourself or allow others to impose upon you. If you want to make £100,000, then write that down – don't write down £50,000 just because you think your true ambition is too difficult to achieve. In the same way, if you want to learn to fly a plane, then don't settle for riding a motorbike just because you think that would be a lot easier.

There are many people who have overcome tremendous odds and even physical and mental disabilities in order to achieve things that often put the rest of us to shame. These amazing people are glowing examples of the fact that perceived limitations can be defied and incredible success achieved if we dare to aim high and think big. So for now, dismiss the words 'I can't', forget any of your old negative beliefs and limitations, and make sure that you aim high and set big goals. After all, as the saying goes, even if you aim for the moon and miss, you'll still be among the stars!

Set deadlines

Every goal you set should be given a fixed deadline. The reason for this is simple. If you don't set a deadline for a goal, the chances are that you will never achieve it. A deadline provides a strong motivation to get things moving now, whereas an open-ended goal carries no such weight. This is why those people who say they will quit smoking 'soon' almost never do, whilst those who set a date to quit – and stick to it – enjoy a far greater success rate.

The deadline you attach to each of your goals is a matter of personal choice, but don't make the mistake of being too easy on yourself. If you know that you could lose a stone in weight in three months, don't give yourself a year to make it happen, because this will only encourage you to delay starting. Similarly, don't go to the other extreme by being too hard on yourself and aiming to lose the weight in three weeks. Doing this would only set you up for failure.

Be prepared to pay the price

There are a few good things in life that can be had for free, but personal success is most certainly not one of them. In order to achieve any goal you set for yourself, there is always a price you will have to pay. In order to succeed, you have to be prepared to put in whatever money and effort are involved. For example, if you set a goal to learn to fly a plane, you will need to put up a large amount of money to pay for flying lessons; you will also have to invest a great deal of your time, taking those lessons and studying towards becoming a qualified pilot. If you are prepared for these costs, then that's great. If you aren't, then you have to accept the fact that this particular goal isn't one that you are really serious about achieving.

There is nothing wrong with examining a goal, determining the cost involved and then deciding that it's not for you after all. In fact that's quite a wise thing to do, and far better than pretending that you are willing to expend the required effort when deep down you know you aren't.

At this moment, you may not be sure what price you will have to pay in order to achieve a particular goal. Don't worry, because we shall deal with this in the next chapter. For now, just remember that achieving any goal requires an investment of time and effort at the very least, and if you aren't willing to pay the price, the goal may need to be shelved until you decide that you are willing, or it may even need to be abandoned entirely.

Set goals you can control

No matter how specific you are, or what kind of deadline you set, setting a goal such as 'I am going to win the National Lottery by 30 June' just isn't a wise thing to do. Every goal you set must be one that you can personally control. Goals such as losing weight, making more money, breaking a sales record, writing a book and quitting smoking are all valid because you have the power to make all of these things happen. Sadly, goals such as winning the lottery or football pools or being named Rear of the Year by a national magazine aren't valid simply because you don't have any control over these things.

There is a simple rule of thumb to follow here: if a goal can be achieved by relying on your personal efforts and abilities, then it is perfectly acceptable. If it can only be achieved through luck, random events or some other influence beyond your control, then it isn't something you should try to pursue further.

CREATING A BLUEPRINT FOR YOUR FUTURE LIFE

Now that we have discussed the general guidelines for setting goals, it is time for you to decide once and for all **exactly** what you want to achieve in the seven main areas of your life. Take a pad and a pen or pencil and go off to a quiet place where you won't be disturbed for at least half an hour. Make yourself comfortable, then write down your answers to the following questions. At this stage don't be concerned about **how** you will achieve your goals, just concentrate on making a start by setting them. Those parts of the equation will be discussed fully in later chapters. Answer each question as fully as possible.

What do I want to achieve in my financial life?

Your goal may be to get out of debt, have a certain sum saved or invested for the future, or to achieve financial independence. Whatever your particular aims are, be specific and write down exactly how much money you want and why, then set a deadline that you believe is appropriate for accumulating this sum.

What do I want to achieve in terms of health and fitness?

Do you want to lose weight? Build muscle? Tone up your abdominals? Have more energy? Quit smoking? Whatever you want to achieve in the area of personal health and fitness, write it down. Be specific and set a date by which you want to succeed.

What goal would I like to set for my career?

It could be to get a new job, start your own business, learn a new profession, or even take early retirement. In short, anything you would like to achieve in your career should be stated here.

What do I want from my personal relationships?

This category of goal refers to your romantic relationships and friendships (family relationships come later). Such goals could be to make a long-term commitment, enjoy a more adventurous sex life, make new friends and so on.

Remember that your goals must be within your control. You can't force other people to make a commitment to you or to get along with you, so make sure your goals in this area are ones that **you** have the power to achieve.

How would I like to feel on a day-to-day basis?

Here we are talking about your emotional life. Would you like to feel happier, more secure, less stressed or more confident? Contrary to what most people believe, you really can change the way you feel every day, and Chapter 8 will show you how, so make a start right now by deciding what changes you would like to make as far as your emotional life is concerned.

What goals do I want to set for my family life?

People often set goals for their finances and careers, but few ever think about setting goals for their family lives. Instead they let this happen by chance, and then wonder why it isn't as good as they want it to be. You can avoid this mistake by setting a goal right now for any improvements you would like to make in your family life. Would you like to get out together more often, or be able to communicate with family members more effectively? Whatever your family-centred goals are, write them down here.

What do I want in the way of spiritual fulfilment?

The word 'spiritual' in this instance simply refers to a sense of connection with the universe at large and doesn't imply any specific religious belief or affiliation. Goals in this area of life should therefore reflect your personal beliefs and practices, or practices that you would like to adopt. These might include joining a group of like-minded people, meditating on a regular basis, or simply enjoying a quiet time alone with your thoughts for half an hour each day.

By answering these questions, you will have established a number of different goals. Go over them once more to ensure that they meet the criteria we discussed earlier (that they are honest, specific, have a deadline attached and so on). You can now allow yourself to feel a certain satisfaction. By completing this exercise, you have joined the most successful three per cent of the population. All you need to do now is learn how to turn those goals into realities in your life.

Making It Happen

As important as goal-setting is, merely having goals does not ensure that you will achieve the success you desire. A written goal is not some kind of magic talisman whereby whatever you set your heart on manifests itself in your life out of thin air. So what makes the difference between the person who achieves their goals and the person who doesn't? The answer can be summarised in a single word: lifestyle. The only difference between those who achieve their goals and those who don't is the way they live each and every day. Destiny does not determine your lifestyle. Your lifestyle determines your destiny.

The vast majority of people who aspire to success in life aspire to a particular kind of success. They see successful people on TV, at the cinema or even amongst their acquaintances; they look at the wealth, the fame, the physique, the career success, the fulfilling relationships and all the other 'results' of success, and they think, 'I want **that**'. But they don't look at the kind of lifestyle that led to that success. If they did, they would realise that none of these successful results can be had without the successful lifestyle that precedes them.

Get this point clear in your mind right now: **you can have any kind of success you desire – if you are willing to adopt the kind of lifestyle that precedes that success.**

I meet many people who, on discovering that I am a writer, tell me that they too have always wanted to write. 'I'd love to write a book,' they say, 'It must be absolutely wonderful to have your name in print and receive those royalty cheques.!'

If you put my life in those terms, then I have to agree. It would be absolutely wonderful to spend my life doing nothing more than getting ideas, having my name put in print and collecting the money.

Unfortunately for the dreamers, there is a lifestyle that precedes all of those results. For example, at five o'clock this morning when everyone else was cosily tucked up in bed, I was in the shower. At 5.15, I was eating a bowl of breakfast cereal. And at 5.30 I was sitting at my desk, putting words on paper. I'm still here at 3.30 in the afternoon. And I'll be here for a while yet.

I don't want this to sound as though I dislike my work. The fact is that I love writing. I actually enjoy getting out of bed early in the morning and spending almost all of my day putting words on paper. The point I am trying to make is that if you want success as a writer, you have to live the lifestyle of a writer. And for the most part that means writing, day in and day out.

The same applies to any other form of success. If you want to achieve the goal of being fit and healthy, you need to adopt the kind of lifestyle that places importance on regular exercise and eating habits. If you want to achieve the goal of having strong family relationships, you need to adopt the kind of lifestyle that places importance on regular family gatherings and good communication skills.

Once again, remember. **Destiny does not determine your lifestyle. Your lifestyle determines your destiny.**

If you compare this strategy with the ones contained in the vast majority of self-help titles, you will find their fatal flaw: most self-help systems claim that the lifestyle is the goal, the end result of having achieved success. Wrong! The adoption of a properly planned lifestyle is the **route** to achieving success in the first place. If you still need convincing, then consider this: how did most currently mega-successful people live **before** they achieved the success they now enjoy?

Did Anita Roddick spend five hours every evening watching soap operas or the latest action films on video? Did Catherine Zeta-Jones spend all day watching daytime television and eating cheese puffs? Was Michael Caine content to work in a dead-end job for little money? Was Richard Branson a regular at his local bar, happily watching the evenings pass by with just a few drinking pals and beers close by to keep him awake?

Of course, the answer to all of these questions is No. But aren't these exactly the kind of things that ordinary, unsuccessful people do all the time? And aren't these the kind of things that ordinary, unsuccessful people actually defend when challenged about their lifestyles? Yes!

And there lies the only real difference between the people who achieve their goals and those that don't – in the things that they do, day after day, week after week and month after month.

I realise that all of this sounds incredibly simple, but the fact is that personal success is simple. It may not be easy, but it certainly isn't complicated.

WHERE IS YOUR LIFESTYLE TAKING YOU?

By completing the exercise at the end of the previous chapter and writing down your goals, you have determined once and for all where you want to go in life. Now you need to take a realistic look at your current lifestyle and honestly conclude whether or not it is taking you in the right direction. To do this, write down a list of all the things you do on a daily basis and then alongside each habit describe the destination it is taking you towards. Here are a few examples to get you started:

Habit	Destination
Smoking	Decreased energy, bad breath, less money, early death
Overeating/poor diet	Decreased energy, weight problems, poor health
Regular exercise	Increased energy, improved health, longer life, less depression, more confidence
Daily meditation	Lower stress levels, sense of contentment

When you have completed this exercise, you will be able to see at a glance whether your daily habits are taking you closer to or further away from the goals that you have set for yourself.

Some of you may think you have very few habits and that instead you tend to allow yourself to 'go with the flow' (otherwise known as drifting aimlessly through life). If this applies to you, then although you probably aren't aware of it, you almost certainly have several habits that you simply fail to recognise. You see, when we examine our lives closely, we soon come to realise that a great part of it is habitual, right down to our choice of television programmes, the restaurants we go to, the people we talk to at work and the sports or leisure activities we choose. In fact it could be said that the habits we maintain and the actions we take (or don't take, since doing nothing is as much of a choice as doing something) on a regular basis are the very things that define us as men and women.

We use habits and actions to define other people all the time. 'He's the guy who's always down the betting shop,' one says. 'She's the overweight chain smoker,' another might comment. Whilst these two examples are hardly flattering, they are honest. We define successful people in the same way – by their habits and actions. 'He's the guy who makes £500 a day by trading options on the stock market,' or, 'She's the one with the great body who's at the kick-boxing class every Wednesday and Friday.'

With all of this in mind, it isn't hard to see how goals are achieved – or not achieved. To achieve a goal, you simply have to adopt the habits that will automatically take you closer towards it instead of further away from it.

Imagine two men of the same age and of equal intelligence, talent and background. Both have access to the same opportunities in life. If one lives one kind of lifestyle, and the other lives an alternative lifestyle, then obviously they will go on to achieve different things. (Please note that although I have used men in this example, the principle applies to both sexes, as do all the principles in this book.) If the first man's lifestyle consists of eating junk food, smoking 40 cigarettes a day and watching six hours of television each evening, the odds are that he will live a brief, lazy, boring life. If the other man's lifestyle consists of eating a healthy diet, playing squash three times a week, and spending each evening writing just one page of a novel, the odds are that he will be fit, healthy and eventually complete the novel.

So you see, there is really no mystery as to why some people achieve their goals whilst others don't. Both success and failure are nothing more than natural outcomes determined by the habits that are maintained on a daily basis. Change your habits and you will change your life!

BE, DO, THEN HAVE

Most unsuccessful people believe they need to have something so that they can do something else and so be successful. For example, a woman might want to have a lot of money so that she can spend her time painting and have a career as an artist.

Unfortunately, these people have the concept muddled up. The successful way to achieve any goal is first to be, then to do and finally to have. The having is the result of the being and doing, and placing it at the front of the equation only leads to disappointment.

For example, if you have set a goal to make more money, then first you need to **be** the kind of person who makes more money and then **do** the kind of things that generate more money. Do these two things and the **having** of money (the achievement of your goal) will happen automatically.

The same applies to all of the other goals you have set for yourself. In order to achieve each and every one of them, all you need to do is be the kind of person you need to be, do the kind of things you need to do and you will have the results you want to have.

WHO ARE YOU?

At this point some of you may be thinking, 'How can I possibly be a different kind of person? How can I be the kind of person I need to be? I am who I am!' This sort of reasoning is common, but erroneous.

Of course, it goes without saying that we all have our unique talents, personalities and perspectives, but it isn't what we say that defines us, it's what we do day after day, week after week and month after month. As I mentioned earlier, our habits define us as human beings.

Your character is not therefore something that is fixed and unchangeable. It is made up of many different aspects that you yourself have created through your habits. If you consider yourself to be a lazy person, for example, this is only because you have got into the habit of doing 'lazy person' things. If you start developing 'active person' habits instead, you will gradually re-create your character so that you become an active person.

You have no doubt heard people say things like, 'Fake it until you make it' and 'Act as if you were already successful and you will become successful'. These suggestions are based on the correct assumption that your habits determine your character, and, furthermore, that by changing your habits and the way you live, you will, in effect, transform yourself on a much deeper level.

Knowing that your lifestyle (which is made up of habits) determines your destiny, it is easy to understand how changing your habits will change your future. However, as we said right at the beginning of this book, knowing how to do something and applying that knowledge are two very different things.

BUILDING A BRIDGE TO PERSONAL SUCCESS

In order to set about changing your habits and lifestyle in order to achieve your goals, you must first identify the kind of habits and lifestyle you need to adopt, and to do this you need to build a bridge.

Look through the goals that you wrote down and select the one that you feel you would like to achieve more than any other. For the purposes of this bridge-building discussion we will refer to this particular goal as your Big Dream. It may be related to health and fitness, or to achieving financial success. Whatever the nature of the goal you have selected as your Big Dream, the principles that follow are universal and therefore equally applicable.

Begin by thinking about the major goal that you have just selected. How do you feel about achieving it? It could be that you feel very confident, but this may not actually be the case. Instead, you may feel as though you are standing on one side of a huge abyss and your Big Dream is way over there on the other side. The gap between where you are and where you want to be may look terrifyingly wide, and the drop below horrendously steep. When you think about your Big Dream, words such as 'hopeless' or 'impossible' may spring to mind.

If this is how you react, then take heart. Such feelings are perfectly normal. But do not allow them to dampen your enthusiasm for achieving success. If you do, you will automatically go back to becoming one of the 97 per cent of dreamers, and you will spend the rest of your life wondering what might have been.

This is what the vast majority of people do. They get a Big Dream. Some may even write it down. And then they look at how far away that dream is and think, 'I can't do that – it's far too difficult!' before backing down and waving goodbye to the one thing they wanted more than anything else in the world.

It doesn't have to be that way. Every person on earth who has achieved massive success through their own efforts has, at one time or another, been right where you are now. Like you, these people had a Big Dream. And like you, these people started a long way off from the realisation of that dream. And yet, despite all of this, they all managed to get from one side of the abyss to the other. They all made their dreams come true.

How? The answer is surprisingly simple. They designed a bridge. A bridge that, when crossed, would take them from where they were to where they wanted to be. Not in one giant leap, but in a series of small steps, which they could confidently take one at a time.

The process begins with the Big Dream that you have just selected. Take a long, hard look at that dream and then think of all the ways an individual could feasibly achieve it. When you have plenty of ideas (and in a moment I'll show you how to get those), then the good is sorted out from the bad, the possible from the impossible, and a step-by-step route to success is mapped out in as much detail as possible. Once complete, this route tells you exactly what you must do and what habits you must adopt in order to get from one side of the abyss to the other.

Let me give you an example. Suppose your major goal is to write a best-selling novel and hit the big time as a famous author. After doing a little brainstorming, you come up with some ideas about how you could go about achieving this. Then, you sort through those ideas to design a 'bridge' that you feel confident you can cross if you take things one step at a time. The bridge that you design might read something like this:

1   Study books/take classes on creative writing.

2   Obtain equipment (personal computer, laser printer, etc.).

3   Decide on genre (crime, romance, thriller, etc.).

4   Decide length to the nearest 1,000 words.

5 Develop a good central idea for the story.

6 Develop the characters.

7 Create the main plot and structure.

8 Ensure that the plot is strong and entertaining throughout.

9 Decide how many days you will spend writing the novel.

10 Divide the number of words by the number of days available.

11 Write the required number of words each day, until the novel is completed.

12 Take a couple of weeks off to recharge your batteries.

13 Revise the novel from beginning to end, tightening and polishing your work.

14 Compile a list of agents or publishers who might like the novel.

15 Send a query letter to these people and offer to send them your manuscript.

16 Send the novel to any of these who express an interest.

17 If no interest is shown, go back and repeat steps 14 to 16.

18 In the meantime, start working on a new novel by going back to step 3.

19 When you have a novel published, set up a series of personal appearances.

20 Hype your work in public at least once a month (book-signings, etc.).

Here we have taken a Big Dream of 'Becoming a best-selling author' and we have turned what was an intangible, almost elusive dream into a seriously workable plan of action. Of course, this in itself doesn't make success automatic, because you would now have to follow the plan (more on this later) but at least, for now, you can see exactly how such a dream can come true. In other words, the dream has lost that 'hopeless' or 'impossible' feeling and has now become something that you can seriously see yourself achieving if you are willing to put the necessary work into making it happen.

Okay, so now it's your turn. You have already selected your major goal. Now you're going to take that goal and design a bridge of your own. Your bridge, if constructed properly, will take your own idea of personal success and turn it into a specific and detailed step-by-step plan towards making that idea a reality.

ADOPTING A ROLE MODEL

There are two ways to go about achieving personal success. The first is to start from scratch, make plenty of mistakes and learn what works and what doesn't by trial and error. Although this approach is taken by the vast majority of people, it is by no means the most effective one. The much better alternative is to study the life of someone who has already achieved the goal you have set for yourself and then adopt the same habits and lifestyle that enabled them to succeed. By doing this, you will be adopting a proven approach that is likely to get you where you want to be much more efficiently.

For example, let's imagine that, having never cooked anything in your life, your Big Dream is to bake a great cake. If you take the trial and error approach you will go into the kitchen, get a variety of ingredients together and then start experimenting to see what goes well together and what doesn't. Doing things this way, it will be months, if not years, before you manage to work out how to bake a really good cake. However, if you take the alternative approach of finding a role model who can already bake a great cake, you will save yourself a great deal of wasted time and effort. All you have to do is learn to follow the proven methods of someone such as Gary Rhodes or Delia Smith by studying their books and television shows.

The principle of adopting a role model may sound obvious when it is applied to a goal of baking a cake, but it is just as effective in any other area of life. The first step to achieving your goal is therefore to identify someone who has already achieved the Big Dream you have set for yourself and then define the main habits and actions that this person had to take in order to succeed. To help you do this effectively, go through the questions that follow and write down your answers to them as fully as possible:

Who do I know who has already achieved the goal I have selected as my Big Dream?

This person could be someone you know personally, such as a friend or family member, or it could be someone you know of, such as a famous businessman or celebrity.

How exactly did this person achieve the goal in question?

To discover the answer to this question, and some of the others that follow, you may need to do some research by reading biographies of your role model or, if it is someone you know personally, by asking them questions directly. Don't avoid this research. The more fully developed your answers to these questions are, the more reliable the bridge you come to build will be.

What specific steps did my role model take to succeed?

List all relevant personal habits, and include any specific 'non-habits' that also contributed to the success. For example, if not smoking helped your role model to succeed, then write down 'not smoking', since this is just as much a good habit as smoking regularly is a bad one.

Did my role model have to have any specialist knowledge or skills in order to succeed?

Some goals require formal training, specialist knowledge or certain skills that have to be learned before achievement can be made. If this is the case where your goal is concerned, note down exactly what knowledge or skills are needed for you to succeed.

What advice would my role model give me if I asked the question, 'How can I succeed in the same way as you?'

All too often we know exactly what we need to do in order to achieve our goals, but fail specifically to recognise this knowledge. Writing down the advice that you imagine your role model would provide gives your subconscious a chance to contribute to this exercise.

PLANNING YOUR SUCCESS BRIDGE

When you have answered all of these questions as fully as you are able, take a fresh sheet of paper and head it: 'My bridge to personal success'. Underneath, list every essential step you need to take in order to achieve your goal. The steps should be listed in the order you have to do them. Often, though not always, the first step on a 'success bridge' is the acquisition of more information and knowledge. If, in your case, you have identified that you need more knowledge in order to be confident in achieving your goal, make sure you define what kind of knowledge you need and how you can obtain it. For example, if you want to set up your own business but you don't know how, your first step might be: 'Go to library for books on how to set up a business'.

Bear in mind that when you have gathered the relevant information, your success bridge may later need to be adjusted slightly. You may, for example, discover that you cannot form a limited company until you have obtained application forms from Companies House. In this case, obtaining application forms becomes a step in itself, and will need slotting into your success bridge before the 'Form a limited company' step.

For now, design your success bridge based on the knowledge you currently have. Start with the most elementary step and then proceed to list all the others until you feel that the bridge is complete.

For this exercise to be most effective, you need to be as detailed as possible. It is better to list 50 small steps rather than ten large ones, so break the large ones down as far as you can. Of course, some goals will naturally require only a few steps. As long as you are as detailed as you possibly can be, that's fine. Remember, the aim here is for you to reduce your Big Dream into a series of steps small enough to make you feel confident about tackling them.

I said earlier that destiny does not determine your lifestyle, but that your lifestyle determines your eventual destiny. By creating your own bridge to personal success, you have actually created the blueprint of the lifestyle that you must now adopt in order to get where you want to go. Now you must live that lifestyle. The way to do this can be summed up in three short sentences.

- Break the habits you need to break.

- Develop the habits you need to develop.

- Take the actions you need to take.

Set out in this way, the route to personal success sounds incredibly simple – and it is. But as I have already said, just because something is simple doesn't mean that it is necessarily easy. The fact is that it isn't easy to break old habits and develop new ones in their place, and it isn't always easy to take the actions you know you should take if you want to achieve your goal. However, there are certain psychological strategies and 'tricks' that you can employ to make things just a little less difficult for yourself.

Breaking old habits and developing new ones

These two steps actually go together, for the best strategy to employ when breaking an old habit is not to simply try and dismiss it in the hope that it will go away of its own accord, but to replace it with a new habit that helps rather than hinders. So, if you want to quit smoking, you shouldn't just throw your cigarettes away and claim freedom, but instead actually give yourself a new habit you can turn to when the craving for nicotine returns. The new habit you choose could be anything that is beneficial, but if it is one that actually serves to support the achievement of your goal, so much the better. In this case, you might decide to improve your fitness. Then, whenever you feel like reaching for a cigarette, you could spend three minutes on a treadmill, do ten sit-ups or even just have a glass of water. By doing this, you turn the old habit trigger of cigarette craving into another step towards the achievement of a new goal.

One simple idea that many of the most successful people use to make breaking old habits and developing new ones easier is to post several pictures that represent the achievement of their major goal in strategic positions throughout their home or office. The intention here is that whenever an individual is tempted by an old habit, the sight of the picture will provide renewed motivation to exercise the new habit instead.

For example, let's say that you want to lose weight and get in better shape. One of your current bad habits may be that you tend to raid the fridge whenever you are bored. If this is the case, find a picture of something or someone that symbolises your goal of physical fitness (perhaps a photograph of a well-known model you admire) and tape it to the front of the fridge door. Then, whenever you are tempted to slip back into your old habits, you will see the picture and be forced to make a conscious decision as to whether or not you will allow yourself to indulge.

The key to breaking or making habits successfully is to try to become more conscious of your power of choice rather than just allowing yourself to operate on auto-pilot. This is an important point that you should understand. If you can set up some kind of system, such as placing pictures around your home, that will serve to remind you of your goal whenever you are likely to indulge in a bad habit, you can consciously choose to work on the new habit instead. The more you do this, the more natural the new habit will begin to feel, until eventually you no longer have to make a conscious decision and the new habit occurs automatically.

Of course, none of this makes making and breaking habits easy, but if you genuinely want to achieve the Big Dream you have set yourself, you will find it a lot less difficult than you might currently imagine.

Taking action

We now need to turn our attention to the step of taking action. In creating your bridge to personal success, you have already identified and put in order the steps you need to take to reach your goal. Now, if you are to benefit, you need to make sure that you actually do take those steps, one at a time and in the correct order.

For many people, taking action is the most difficult step of all. This is not usually because the actions required to achieve the majority of goals are difficult in themselves (after all, if you really want to lose weight, how difficult can it be to eat a salad instead of a burger?). The difficulty arises because they require us to step out of our normal comfort zone. Most people hold the mistaken belief that achieving success should be a smooth and comfortable ride, so when it comes to taking any action that makes them feel uncomfortable, they shy away from it.

You must realise right from the outset that it is usually the things that make you feel most uncomfortable that bring the biggest rewards in terms of success and achievement. The man who wants to become a champion bodybuilder must first force himself to take the uncomfortable action of pounding weights day after day, week after week, month after month. The woman who wants to write a novel must force herself to take the uncomfortable action of facing a blank page each day and writing the next section of her story.

There is one good thing about this: if you breach the comfort zone often enough by forcing yourself to take the necessary 'uncomfortable' actions, the zone itself begins to expand so that it encompasses those new actions. In other words, the actions become less and less uncomfortable and, eventually, writing the novel or lifting the weights feels just as natural as watching TV or taking the dog for a walk. This is when the new lifestyle that you deliberately engineered begins to take care of itself and allows you to 'coast' towards the goal you have set out to achieve.

For these reasons, don't allow yourself to avoid taking the 'uncomfortable' steps that you know you need to take. Instead, exercise all the self-discipline you can muster and force yourself to take action, bearing in mind that the stricter you are with yourself, the sooner these beneficial actions will begin to feel more natural, and the faster you will get to your chosen destination.

THE MAGIC KEY: SELF-DISCIPLINE

As you will have gathered by now, if there is any 'magic' responsible for personal success in life, then it is simply the magic of self-discipline. People who set goals, build a bridge towards those goals and then take one step at a time across that bridge, exercising their self-discipline all the while, will undoubtedly succeed. Without that self-discipline, however – even if they set goals and build a bridge of actions they need to take – they won't have a hope of achieving the personal success they desire.

Self-discipline is a lot easier to maintain if you live each day according to a predetermined plan. Most people get up in the morning, live the day and then go to bed no closer to success than they were that morning. They repeat this process day after day, week after week and month after month. Eventually, they sit down and wonder why their life hasn't changed.

Successful people operate differently. They get up in the morning, live the day according to a predetermined plan, and go to bed at least one tiny step closer to success than they were yesterday. They repeat this process day after day, week after week and month after month. Then eventually they sit down and realise that they are actually living the dream they set for themselves in the very beginning.

The key is having the predetermined plan and also the self-discipline to stick to it. Successful people plan not only how they will go about achieving their big dream (as you did when you designed your success bridge) but they also plan each day to ensure that they actually start walking across that bridge. You must do the same. You must forget your old lifestyle and use the bridge you have created to create a whole new lifestyle. And then you must stick to that lifestyle, living it one day at a time.

YOUR LIFESTYLE GRID

To help you do this, you are going to create a 'lifestyle grid', a sort of guide, or timetable, for your daily actions. First, draw a grid on a blank sheet of paper. Across the top, write the days of the week starting with Monday. Write the hours of the day down the left-hand side of the grid, beginning at 7 am and listing each hour until 10 pm. The grid should look something like this.

	Monday	Tuesday	Wednesday
7 am			
8 am			
9 am			
10 am			
11 am			
12 noon			
1 pm			
2 pm			
3 pm			
4 pm			
5 pm			
6 pm			
7 pm			
8 pm			
9 pm			
10 pm			

Thursday	Friday	Saturday	Sunday

This lifestyle grid will ensure that each day takes you at least one small step closer to your Big Dream. All you need to do is complete it and then live your life according to this daily plan.

Enter on the grid all the activities you are currently committed to that are absolutely essential, such as working at your existing job, collecting your children from school, taking a morning shower, shopping for groceries and doing household chores. Do this for every day of the week, and make sure that every item you put on the lifestyle grid is 100 per cent **essential**.

Next, enter the activities that you need to do in order to maintain good relationships with your immediate family, such as spending Sunday afternoon with your children or spending one or two evenings each week (or one or two hours each evening) with your partner. Be realistic when you do this, and be honest with yourself. Remember, no one **needs** to watch television, go to the bridge club or spend Saturday night at the local pub, so these things don't count.

Now take a look at the grid. How much blank space do you have left? This is the amount of time you have on a weekly basis to invest in your future. In other words, the blank spaces represent the time you have available to take the steps you listed when designing your success bridge.

How you 'slot' these in to your lifestyle grid is entirely up to you, but you must ensure that every day of the week you do something that will help take you closer to your Big Dream. Refer back to your success bridge to identify the particular actions that you personally need to take in order to achieve your particular goal.

For example, if you aspire to being a best-selling novelist, you will have already determined that you need time to study, think and write. So, for writing you might allow two hours every evening, Monday through Friday, and four hours on both Saturdays and Sundays. In addition, you could schedule two hours for study time on Monday and Tuesday and an hour and a half of thinking time on Wednesday and Thursday.

Of course, this is just an illustration, but look at what you've done. You have taken your week and set aside 25 hours that you can now devote to the realisation of your Big Dream. That's the equivalent of more than three working days each and every week! Over the course of a year, you will spend a massive 1,300 hours dedicating yourself to success as a novelist, which equates to more than 162 working days!

This is the science of personal success in action! No fuzzy theories or dubious promises – just a brand-new lifestyle that you have designed to take you to your major goal.

Unless you are already working 12-hour days and you genuinely don't have the time, I strongly suggest that you aim to spend at least 25 hours per week working towards your Big Dream. When you consider the fact that the average person watches over 30 hours of television each week, this really shouldn't be a problem as long as you are prepared to sacrifice allegiance to the tube in order to give yourself the chance to live the life of your dreams.

If you have time left over after allocating 25 hours to the achievement of your major goal, you can use it as you wish. Slot in some recreation time. Maybe 30 minutes of exercise each day. Or, if you wish, you can spend even more time on your major goal.

How you use the lifestyle grid is, at the end of the day, entirely up to you. But remember the master concept: **your lifestyle determines your destiny.** If your lifestyle concentrates heavily on you working towards success, then success is what you will get. If, however, you decide that television, bridge clubs and the local pub are more important, then that kind of lifestyle will not speed your path to success. Which is fine if it's your choice, but just don't complain that success is a matter of luck, fate or some other external variable, because you now know deep down inside that this just isn't true.

To end this section, I have included a fully completed lifestyle grid that is based on one that a friend of mine created. I have put the 'success lifestyle' aspects of his grid in bold letters so that you can see at a glance how much time he committed to his major goal. This, by the way, was 'To become a published author', and yes, he did succeed. It took 19 months from the creation of his grid to the attainment of his Big Dream, but in his words, 'The time flew by, and the experience was incredible. I wasn't just **waiting** to be a writer – the grid enabled me to start **living** as a writer.'

Use this example to inspire your own lifestyle grid based on the materials you prepared when you created your bridge to success. Then exercise your self-discipline and live by the grid. Do this, and success will be yours for the taking.

	Monday	Tuesday	Wednesday
7 am	Exercise	Exercise	Exercise
8 am	Shower	Shower	Shower
9 am	Work	Work	Work
10 am	Work	Work	Work
11 am	Work	Work	Work
12 noon	Work	Work	Work
1 pm	**Study**	**Think**	**Study**
2 pm	Work	Work	Work
3 pm	Work	Work	Work
4 pm	Work	Work	Work
5 pm	Free	Free	Free
6 pm	**Write**	**Write**	**Write**
7 pm	**Write**	**Write**	**Write**
8 pm	**Write**	**Write**	**Write**
9 pm	Free	Free	Free
10 pm	Free	Free	Free

Thursday	Friday	Saturday	Sunday
Exercise	Exercise	Exercise	Exercise
Shower	Shower	Shower	Shower
Work	Work	**Write**	**Write**
Work	Work	**Write**	**Write**
Work	Work	**Write**	**Write**
Work	Work	**Write**	**Write**
Think	**Study**	Free	Free
Work	Work	Free	Free
Work	Work	Free	Free
Work	Work	Free	Free
Free	Free	Free	Free
Write	**Write**	Free	Free
Write	**Write**	Free	Free
Write	**Write**	Free	Free
Free	Free	Free	Free
Free	Free	Free	Free

Summary of Part 1

I have now explained all the principles of achieving personal success that you need to learn. To summarise, the steps you need to take to achieve any goal in life are as follows:

- Write your goal down, ensuring that it is specific and that you can control the outcome.

- Set a deadline for your goal.

- Build a success bridge by writing down all the steps you need to take in order to get from where you are to where you want to be. Include details of any habits you need to adopt and any that you need to break.

- Create a lifestyle grid to help you organise your time effectively and ensure that every day takes you at least one step closer to the achievement of your goal.

Understanding and using these principles will certainly enable you to get whatever you want out of life. However, to help you even further, we will now move on to Part 2 of this book, which details the specific actions you need to take to achieve success in seven areas: finances, physical health and fitness, career, relationships, emotions, family and spirituality.

Part 2

APPLYING THE SCIENCE

Financial Success

*I*n today's busy world, money is viewed as something magical. It is seen as something that has the power to change lives, solve problems and literally buy us freedom from the nine-to-five rat-race of having to earn a living. That said, it's no wonder that the number one goal of many people is simply to make as much money as possible.

Unfortunately, this particular goal can actually make our lives worse rather than better. If we chase money for its own sake, then we can soon find ourselves working long, hard hours, day after day, in order to maintain a lifestyle that we never really have the time to enjoy. Of course, when we die we'll get to leave a lot of expensive stuff behind, but that isn't really the point, is it?

This chapter is headed Financial Success. What this term means to you will depend largely on your current status. If you are struggling with debts that seem to get bigger and bigger each month, then for you financial success might be clearing those debts and living the rest of your life without having to borrow another penny. If you are already debt-free, then financial success might mean ensuring that you have enough to live on when you retire. Still others among you might equate financial success with taking your investment portfolio into six figures.

However you define financial success, this chapter will help you to achieve your goals. It will also help to ensure that you get into the habit of controlling your money, rather than allowing your money to control you.

WHAT DOES FINANCIAL SUCCESS MEAN TO YOU?

We have already established that the first step to accomplishing anything in life is to define your goal as clearly as possible, so let's apply this step to your finances. What exactly do you want in this area of your life? What goal would you need to achieve to feel financially successful?

Below I have given some sample responses to these questions. However, there are really no right or wrong answers to these questions, because we are all unique and we all have different ambitions, hopes and dreams. There are many other responses, so feel free to throw convention to the wind and come up with whatever applies to you.

- I want to be free of all debts, including the mortgage.

- I want to have £x set aside in a savings account.

- I want to be able to travel the world when I retire.

- I want a new car every two years.

- I want to be able to give my daughter the wedding of her dreams.

- I want two foreign holidays each year.

- I want to have more control over my spending habits.

Spend as long as you like defining exactly what it would take for you to feel financially successful, then pick the most important thing that you want and make it your main goal. For example, if you want to clear debts of £8,000 and you also want £10,000 in savings, your main goal would be to clear the £8,000 debts. When that goal is reached, you can then move on to getting the £10,000 savings together.

Write your main goal down on paper, then set a deadline for its achievement that seems reasonable to you. Remember that you must be sure that you can control your outcome. If your goal involves making more money, or spending less, or is a combination of the two, then it is well within your sphere of influence and can undoubtedly be achieved. If, however, your goal is to become a pools jackpot winner, go back and read Part I of this book again – you weren't paying attention!

Now that you have your goal for financial success, write down all of the reasons why you want to achieve it. These reasons will provide you with the long-term motivation you need to make it happen, and they can be as personal (and silly) as you like, since no one else need ever read what you've written.

For example, let's imagine that your goal is to become debt-free within two years. Your reasons might include any – or all – of the following:

- I'll be able to sleep at night because I won't owe anyone a penny.

- My partner will feel less pressured to work long hours.

- I'll have finally faced up to my debts – and conquered them.

- I'll feel 'clean'.

- I'll feel free to get on with the rest of my life.

When you have written down plenty of good reasons for why you want and need to achieve your goal, you can proceed to the next stage.

IDENTIFY THE REQUIRED ACTIONS

It may surprise you, but no matter what kind of financial goal you have set for yourself, its attainment will involve only three major actions:

- Increasing your income

- Controlling your expenditure

- Putting the resulting surplus to good use.

If you want to become debt-free, then that 'good use' of surplus would be paying off your debts month by month. If your goal is to have £10,000 in a savings account, then the 'good use' would be saving your surplus month by month, and so on. The size of your goal, in monetary terms, is largely irrelevant. Successful achievement of financial goals still comes down to the same three major actions.

If you aren't convinced of this, then consider this example. A man who currently earns £15,000 each year has set a goal to have £100,000 in the bank within the next 15 years. This may sound rather a lot to aim for, but it is in fact easily achievable just by implementing the three major actions. All he has to do is:

- Increase his income by 10 per cent each year.

- Save 20 per cent of all he earns by controlling his expenditure.

- Invest his savings wisely to generate a 5 per cent annual return.

If he does these three things then here is how he would progress towards his goal year by year . . .

Year	Income	Save 20%	Total saved	Yield 5%	New total
01	£ 15,000	£ 3,000	£ 3,000	£ 150	£ 3,150
02	16,500	3,300	6,450	322	6,772
03	18,150	3,630	10,402	520	10,922
04	19,965	3,993	14,915	745	15,660
05	21,961	4,392	20,052	1,002	21,054
06	24,157	4,831	25,885	1,294	27,179
07	26,572	5,314	32,493	1,624	34,117
08	29,229	5,845	39,962	1,998	41,960
09	32,151	6,430	48,390	2,419	50,809
10	35,366	7,073	57,882	2,894	60,776
11	38,902	7,780	68,556	3,427	71,983
12	42,792	8,558	80,541	4,027	76,010
13	47,071	9,414	85,424	4,271	89,695
14	51,778	10,355	100,050	5,002	105,052

As you can see, the goal of saving £100,000 within 15 years is achieved quite comfortably; in fact, it is achieved with a whole year to spare.

Of course, this illustration assumes that you can get an average annual return of 5 per cent on your savings. In the real world, you will sometimes get more, and sometimes less, depending on fluctuations in the global economy (and thus in interest rates) due to current affairs. However, this illustration does show what is possible, and how incredibly effective the three major actions really can be when they are applied **habitually**.

Obviously, we can't stop at simply proving the point. Knowing roughly what you should be doing isn't the same as knowing exactly how to do it. So let's now look at each of the three major 'wealth actions' in more detail.

Action 1: Increase your income

Increasing your income isn't a complicated matter. In fact, if you discard the possibility of generating income from existing investments, you have just three options: get a pay rise, find a new job with a higher salary or start a business of your own in your spare time.

Get a pay rise

Perhaps the simplest way of increasing your income is to get a pay rise from your current employer. Most people in full-time employment expect an annual pay rise, but usually such rises only serve to keep your income in line with the rising cost of living – they don't often take into account your true value as an employee.

'Value' is the operative word here. Unless you are genuinely valuable to your employer then you aren't likely to get anything more than the average, standard annual raise. That said, your first task is to ensure that you do more than you are currently paid to do. Break free of the 'I just work here' mentality and start seeing yourself as an individual who creates value and contributes to the bottom line of the company you work for. Then find ways to excel in this role. Work more efficiently, be more dedicated than your colleagues and perform every task with an eye on quality.

When you get into this habit of going the extra mile, your employer will soon start noticing how much you contribute to his organisation. At this point he may in fact call you into his office and offer you a pay rise or promotion so that you can start adding even more value to his cause. If he doesn't, you'll need to ask directly for what you want.

However, simply walking into your employer's office and asking for a pay rise isn't usually the best way to accomplish the goal. Lots of people do that, and your employer is probably used to people wanting more money. So you must set yourself apart from the masses. Don't beg for anything. Instead, prepare a written report of all the different ways in which you add value to the company, then present this to your employer in private and ask for what you want. Be friendly and confident. After all, you aren't asking for blood. You are only asking for what you feel you genuinely deserve.

It is often a good idea to ask for slightly more than you would be happy to get. Employers often feel that everything is negotiable, and could possibly try to reach a compromise with you. By exaggerating your request, you can allow yourself to go along with this, and your employer will be content, thinking that he's actually saved money in giving you a slightly smaller rise.

As long as you have genuinely added value to your company, there is no reason why you shouldn't get a reasonable pay rise when you ask for it in the manner described. If you don't, then you should seriously consider moving to another company where your skills are likely to be better appreciated and rewarded.

Find a new job

The second way to increase your income is to find a new job that pays more than your current position. This might sound a little extreme, and it is true that changing jobs may take you out of your comfort zone, but complacency never got anyone anywhere, and it certainly isn't something that will take you towards financial success. If you have asked for a pay rise and been refused, finding a new job is an option that you should give some serious consideration. Equally, if you know that your current job just isn't going to provide you with an environment in which you can grow and progress – in terms of both personal fulfilment and financial success – then you should consider taking your talents elsewhere.

The best time to find a new job is whilst you are already employed, so don't make the mistake of quitting your current position unless you have already lined up a better one. Instead, think carefully about the kind of new position you want and what salary you would like, then start looking around for opportunities that appear to be suitable. Attend interviews during lunch hours or during other spare periods, and when you have landed the job you want, serve your notice and leave.

It is unlikely that you will ever find a position that you find completely fulfilling, so don't wait for a 'perfect' opportunity to come along before you make your move. At the same time, don't change jobs just for the sake of it. If a new position doesn't provide more money for your skills, or doesn't offer at least as much potential satisfaction as the one you are in, sit tight until you find one that does.

Start a business of your own

If you are the kind of person who will never be satisfied to any degree working for someone else, the third option you have is to start a business of your own. This may well take you even further out of your comfort zone, but as in all areas of life, the more daring you are, the more potential benefits there are to be gained.

Starting your own business puts you in a position where you truly can earn what you are worth. If you work hard and succeed, you could increase your current income as an employee many times over. Running your own business has other advantages too:

- You can choose your own hours and fit your work around other things that are important to you, such as spending time with your family or being able to visit the gym on a regular basis.

- You can choose to generate your income by doing something you really enjoy, so that work becomes fulfilling in its own right. For example, if you enjoy playing the piano, you could become a piano teacher and spend your working life sharing your passion with others.

- You truly become the master of your own destiny. You decide how you want your career to unfold, what direction you go in and how much income you generate. This kind of freedom simply isn't possible as an employee.

With so many great advantages to self-employment, you may be asking yourself why more people don't take the plunge and start their own businesses. The number one reason is probably a fear of failure. Most people don't want to risk leaving the relative security of working for someone else in order to take full responsibility for their lives and possibly fail in the process. In addition, those who are prepared to take the plunge tend to put off doing so until they feel the time is right – that is, until external conditions are perfect for self-employment and the risk inherent in taking such a step is as small as possible.

Unfortunately, conditions are never perfect for starting your own business, and doing so always involves an element of risk, so the vast majority of people remain in positions of employment more out of fear rather than out of a genuine desire to remain employed.

The good news is that there is no law that states that you have to make starting your own business an 'all or nothing' gamble. It is perfectly possible to start a business of your own in a small way in your spare time, thereby retaining the perceived security of your employed position until it becomes apparent that your own business really can provide all that you need – and more besides.

You may find it hard to decide what kind of business to start. There are obviously many different forms of self-employment, and no single business opportunity is equally suited to all people. However, there are three main approaches to setting up your own business that have proven time and time again to be very effective. Take one of these routes into self-employment and the chances of you succeeding are high – as long as you work hard and invest time and effort into achieving success.

Go freelance

The first route into self-employment is to carry out your current work on a freelance basis. For example, if you drive cabs for a taxi company, you could set up your own company and drive your own cab, then expand as you succeed and eventually get others to do the driving. Or, to give you another example, if you currently work in a bakery making wedding cakes, you could set yourself up as a freelance provider of wedding cakes.

The advantages of going freelance are numerous:

- Instead of receiving the same salary month after month regardless of how good you are at your job, you get to keep all of the profits that your efforts generate.

- You will enjoy your work a lot more if you know that you are doing it for yourself rather than for an employer.

- As you serve your clients in a satisfactory way, you can ask for personal recommendations and expand your client base at an exponential rate.

- If you ever get more clients than you can personally handle, you can employ other talented individuals to help you meet the demand.

Turn a hobby into a business

The second proven way of starting a business of your own is to look to your hobbies and interests and think about whether any of them could be turned into a way of generating profit. The vast majority of hobbies can be transformed into profit-making ventures. Here are a few examples to inspire you:

- If you have a passion for astronomy, you can turn this into a successful business selling astronomical telescopes, charts, books and other items.

- If you are a keep fit enthusiast, start teaching fitness classes or become a personal trainer.

- If you are a keen (and proficient) amateur photographer, you could make a great living as a wedding photographer, later branching out into in-home family portraits and possibly setting up a private studio.

There are thousands of ways to turn hobbies and interests into successful businesses, and the chances are that you already have the seeds of self-employed success just waiting to be discovered and germinated. Think about what you like to do in your spare time, consider how you can get paid to do it – then start doing it!

Work on commission

The third main way of becoming self-employed is to offer to sell products and services on a commission basis. Many people hate the idea of commission-based sales work, but the fact is that if you are good with people you can make a tremendous amount of money through commissions.

The world of commission-based sales is not limited to double-glazing and insurance companies; it includes many other products and services that, generally speaking, aren't very difficult to sell. Perfumes, cleaning products, cosmetics, costume jewellery and books are all commonly sold via independent agents who take a percentage of sales as their income. The more products they sell, the more money they make. It really is as simple as that.

A growing trend is for some companies to teach agents how to become team leaders and form their own sales force of self-employed salespeople. This so-called 'multi-level marketing' enables you to profit not only from what you sell, but also from the sales of the people in your team. Whilst many people confuse this marketing arrangement with the infamous pyramid selling scams of the 1970s, they are really a world apart and many highly respected companies now offer MLM opportunities for just a tiny initial investment.

Making money by selling the products and services of others – and possibly building a sales force of your own – is not something that appeals to everyone. However, if you have an outgoing personality and like the idea of meeting new people on a daily basis, commission-based sales is something you should definitely investigate further.

From what you have read thus far, it should be apparent that there are many ways in which you can increase your income. The opportunities available to you are immense. But you will never make more money by simply wishing for more. You need to decide exactly how you want to go about it, and then take the required actions.

Action 2: Control your expenditure

It is no good increasing your income if all you do is increase your spending at the same time. To become a financial success you need to increase your income whilst at the same time controlling your expenditure. This effectively enables you to generate a substantial 'surplus' that you can then use wisely to attain your main financial goal, whatever that may be.

Controlling your expenditure is not difficult, but, as with so many things, it does require a degree of planning and self-discipline. The first step is to learn how to budget.

Drawing up a budget

The word 'budget' isn't something that tends to excite people. To the vast majority, it brings to mind a grey existence marked by penny-pinching and miserly attitudes. A budget viewed in this way... well, it just isn't sexy.

Fortunately, budgeting doesn't have to be seen in this way. A budget can also be viewed as a blueprint for wealth that, if adhered to, can make all of your financial dreams come true. This, I think you'll agree, is a much more empowering attitude, and gives the word 'budget' a whole new feel.

Quite simply, a budget is a spending plan. You start by calculating how much money you have coming into your life, and then budget, or allocate, how that money will be spent. Spending money therefore becomes something that you do consciously, according to a predetermined plan, rather than something you do unconsciously or according to how you happen to feel emotionally on any given day.

Creating your budget

Start by calculating your current monthly income after all taxes have been paid. If you have a salary, then this will be easy – just write down your take-home pay. If you are on commission or you are self-employed, simply write down your average monthly income, minus the figure you set aside for income tax purposes. Add to this figure any other income you receive, such as interest from savings, government benefits, and so on. The final total should be the amount of money that comes into your possession every month.

When you have done this, calculate how much you must spend on essential supplies and services. These include:

- Rent or mortgage payments
- Electricity, gas and other fuels
- Council tax
- Food and groceries
- Clothes
- Travel to/from work
- Telephone
- School fees/lunch money, etc.

- Petrol/car expenses.

- Loan /hire purchase/credit card payments

The items in this list should not include anything you do for pleasure or luxury items, so if you've allowed for a weekly bottle of champagne or a night out at the pub in your food and groceries section, go back and take it out.

Now add up all of these essential outgoings and, hopefully, you will find that you have a surplus of money. Often, this surplus will be a lot higher than you may have originally anticipated, since we haven't taken into account what you spend on non-essentials. If your outgoings even at this stage exceed your income (perhaps because of large debts), then you have a major problem and you should take immediate action to put things right. A good way to start is by discussing your circumstances with someone at your local Citizens' Advice Bureau. And, of course, you can aim to increase your income using any of the approaches we discussed earlier in this chapter.

Assuming that your income does exceed your outgoings at this stage, you now have to decide how much of this surplus you will allow yourself to spend on entertainment and other luxuries. Most people, unaware of what their surplus actually is, spend all of it on daily extravagances, only to find that when they want to use money for something more substantial, there isn't any left. You need to decide right here at the outset how much you want to spend on the fun things in life, be it £10, £30 or £100 each week.

Before you make this decision, remember that if you want jam tomorrow, you can't spend too much today. If you want to achieve your financial goal as quickly and effectively as possible, you should be modest in allocating money for today's luxuries. Of course, this might mean that you have to make a few sacrifices for the time being, but in the long run such sacrifices are almost always worthwhile.

If you are budgeting for a household rather than just for yourself as an individual, you should discuss luxury and entertainment spending with others who will be affected by your decisions. And don't think that all entertainment spending is necessarily frivolous. For example, if you have children who need money each week to go swimming or take part in any other useful activities, try to ensure that these things can continue. Forcing others to make sacrifices on your behalf is not a good way to make your budget work. For a budget to be effective, it needs to be acceptable to everyone who is involved.

When you have drawn up your budget in this way, you should have a surplus of money left over, even after taking into account entertainment and luxury items. I will show you how you can put this surplus to the best possible use in a few moments, but first I would like to discuss several ways to increase the amount even more by reducing the cost of your existing financial commitments.

Getting more bang for your buck

We live in a capitalist society, and getting more from your money is not as difficult as most people seem to think. Competition is fierce in all areas of business, and by looking around for cheaper and better deals on everything from your mortgage to your car insurance, you can effectively increase the amount of money that is left over for you to use in other ways.

The key to this is to regularly shop around and ensure that you have the best deals on all of your major expenses. Many expenses can be reduced by investing a little time and effort in this way. The list below is by no means exhaustive, but will help you to get started and could well increase your surplus substantially.

- Get a different mortgage. If you have been with your current mortgage company for three years or more and are able to switch to a different lender, look around for more attractive deals. The chances are that there is money to be saved in moving to a different company and in some cases you could save hundreds of pounds even on an annual basis.

- If you have insurance policies for your car, home or contents that you haven't reviewed for two years or more, take a look around to see what else is currently on offer. It has been estimated that more than 80 per cent of people waste money on insurance simply because they can't be bothered to search for better deals. Don't be one of them!

- If you have outstanding balances on credit cards, find out what rate of interest you are currently paying and then see if you can reduce this by switching to a different company. Alternatively, reduce your credit card interest by taking out a personal loan at a low rate and using this to clear the credit cards. However, do not continue to use the credit cards or you'll get yourself into an even worse situation.

There are many other ways in which you can increase your surplus by aiming to get better deals on current commitments, but I'll leave it to you to become a 'value sleuth' and do the necessary homework. Just remember, before you spend any money on major purchases, always ask yourself if you can get the same product or service cheaper elsewhere. If you can't, so be it. But if you can, you know what you should do.

Action 3: Put your surplus to good use

By increasing your income and controlling your expenditure in the ways I have described, you should have a healthy surplus that you are now able to put to good use. What that 'good use' is will depend on your personal financial success goal.

● If your goal is to eliminate debt, then you should take 80 per cent of your final surplus (i.e. after everything, including luxuries, has been budgeted for) and use it to pay off debts in their order of importance. The remaining 20 per cent should be saved or invested for your own financial security (I will deal with this shortly).

● If you are already debt-free (apart from a mortgage), then 100 per cent of your final surplus should be saved or invested according to the guidelines that follow.

There are three basic ways of making your money grow. You can save your money in a normal interest-bearing deposit account with a bank or building society; you can invest indirectly in the stock market; or you can invest directly in the stock market.

Deposit accounts

These are the simplest of all savings vehicles and are offered by banks, building societies and other financial institutions as a way to gain interest on finances that aren't being used. Accounts can generally be opened with a minimal balance (many can be opened with less than £10) and they are probably as safe a home as you can get for your money. The only risk you run is that of the account provider going out of business (and even then, a large part of your money will be insured against such an occurrence).

The downside of deposit accounts is their low interest rates. These obviously vary according to the underlying base rate of interest, but generally speaking, the best you can hope for money in a deposit account is that it keeps up with the rate of inflation.

If you aren't used to saving, then deposit accounts could be a good place to start, but they aren't the most effective way of making your money grow by any means.

Indirect stock market investment

When viewed over the longer term, the stock market traditionally offers the best environment for growth as far as savings and investments are concerned. In good times, the UK stock market has provided average returns of over ten per cent each year. Of course, in bad times, stock markets can go down quite dramatically too, but over the long term, balanced and careful stock market investment almost always reaps better rewards than deposit accounts.

Of course, profiting from the stock market isn't something you can do with your eyes closed. To make your money grow, you need to know which stocks and shares to invest in, and, equally importantly, when you should sell those investments in order to 'lock in' profits that have already been generated.

If you don't have the required level of expertise, or you would like someone else to make your investment decisions on your behalf, you may like to consider indirect investment in the stock market. This is where you invest your money into a special investment fund (a mutual fund, unit trust, ISA, etc.) and allow the managing company to pool your money with that of other investors and aim to generate profits on the whole amount. Profits are then shared pro rata between investors at the end of each investment period (usually every year). Fund management companies generally take a commission on these profits, so they have a clear incentive to generate profits, and over recent years the performance of some funds has been astounding.

Indirect stock market investment funds come in all shapes and sizes, and to suit all kinds of investors. Some funds 'lock in' profits each year to provide the investor with a certain amount of guaranteed return on their money. Others ride the stock market roller coaster without locking in profits, and this means that you could get back less than you invest if things don't go to plan. Because there are so many different options to choose from, and because legislation changes all the time regarding investment funds, you should seek the advice of an independent professional financial adviser before you commit yourself to anything. If at this stage you would simply like to learn more about how the stock market works, then you might consider studying my series of financial books, including *Understand Shares In A Day*, which is available from all good bookshops.

Direct stock market investment

If you have the knowledge, or the inclination to acquire the knowledge, then the third way of making your final surplus grow could be open to you, and this is the way of direct stock market investment. As a direct investor you would buy and sell your own shares (or possibly other financial vehicles such as traded options or futures) via a professional broker. Potential profits in this arena are virtually unlimited, but then so are the potential losses. It is therefore vital that you know what you are doing if you intend to succeed in making money rather than losing the surplus you already have – and possibly more besides.

For those of you who wish to learn the ropes of successful investment in stocks and shares there are many books on the subject, as I mentioned in the previous section, and there are specialist training courses and seminars that you can attend to get the know-how you need. Explore the subject further and then, if you decide to go for it, do so with caution, using the other two forms of money growth as you gain expertise and confidence.

FINANCIAL SUCCESS – YOURS FOR THE TAKING

When I said earlier in this chapter that financial success comes down doing just three things – increasing your income, controlling your expenditure and putting the surplus to good use – you may well have had your doubts. By now I hope that you agree with me, and that you have come to understand that achieving financial success really isn't all that difficult.

As I said in the first part of this book, achieving almost anything is quite simple as long as you define your goal, find out how to achieve it and then take the necessary actions you need to take in order to get where you want to go.

Follow the three action steps that I have outlined as your plan and financial success – whatever that may mean to you – really is yours for the taking!

Health and Fitness

The last 20 years have seen enormous growth in the health and fitness industry. Gym memberships have soared, home exercise equipment sells by the truckload and there are thousands of diet, fitness and exercise books and videos on the market. Yet despite all of this, obesity is on the increase, levels of health aren't improving much and few people are really happy with the way they look.

Once again, this is because knowing what to do and actually doing it are two different things. Fad diets may work for a while, but too often when the diet comes to an end, the previous unhealthy lifestyle comes back into play and the weight goes back on. Home exercise gadgets and gizmos catch your attention and seem fun for a while, but all too soon the novelty of using them wears off, the equipment gets stored away to gather dust and you are left with yet another shattered dream to nurse.

Many people dabble with health and fitness in this way for their whole lives, never quite getting to where they want to go. The reason for this is simple: we believe there's always a short cut to success. And there isn't.

There is no magic secret to becoming healthy and physically fit. You don't need a gym membership that costs several hundred pounds, you don't need expensive exercise equipment, and a healthy diet, contrary to popular opinion, is no more expensive than an unhealthy one. High levels of health and fitness are available to all of us, if we are willing to adopt the right kind of lifestyle.

You already know that in order to have, you first need to be and do, so what do you need to be and do in order to have a great level of health and fitness? I'm glad you asked that, because the whole of this chapter is devoted to giving you the answer.

BE HONEST WITH YOURSELF

The first thing you need to be is honest. Be honest with yourself about your current level of health and fitness. This sounds obvious, but the vast majority of people who really need to take action spend most of their time creating excuses for their lack of health and fitness, rather than honestly facing facts. Instead of admitting that they are fat, people say that they are 'big boned', 'cuddly' or have a 'thyroid problem'. Of course, in some cases there can be a medical condition that makes it difficult for a person to achieve health and fitness, but 99 times out of 100, such excuses are just that – excuses.

I don't mean to be hard on you here, but I do need to be forceful. Unless you can take a really good, objective look at yourself and be totally honest in evaluating your current levels of health and fitness, the chances of you becoming more healthy and increasingly fit are virtually nil.

The best way of enforcing honesty on yourself is to get someone to take a picture of you either fully naked or in a swimsuit, and get it developed. If you can't bear the thought of some chap in a lab seeing you in all of your natural glory, get a Polaroid camera and take the picture using that. Either way, get hold of a full colour photograph of you wearing as little as possible whilst standing in a natural pose. In other words, there's to be no sucking-in of the gut or pushing-out of the chest.

When you get the picture, sit down and take a good look at it. I guarantee that unless you already enjoy high levels of health and fitness, you won't like what you see. Every day we look at ourselves in the mirror or in photos, where we are aiming to look our best, but very rarely do we ever get to see what we really look like to other people. When we finally see a photo of ourselves as we really are, the response is generally one of shock.

This is good, for it forces you to be honest about the way you look to your partner, children, colleagues and peers, and honesty is the first step to changing what you don't want for what you do.

Before you allow your honest frame of mind to wear off, evaluate yourself as though you didn't know the person in the photograph. How healthy and fit does he or she look? Does he have a beer belly? Does she have flabby upper arms? Is there a double chin in the making? What about posture? Is this a person who is confident in their physical appearance, or someone who would rather be fully clothed and preferably hiding behind a large building?

Now think about how the person might look if they took more care of themselves and adopted a healthier lifestyle. What would the guy look with a six-pack instead of a beer belly? How would the woman look if her thighs and buttocks were toned properly? If your opinion is that the individual in the photograph would look better, then you've just reached a turning-point in your pursuit of health and fitness.

No matter what shape you are in right now, your potential is truly incredible. Trapped inside that body of yours is a wonderfully healthy and fit person who is just waiting to be let out. This person within you is sexy, toned, sleek, energetic and vibrant, and looks and feels better than you could possibly imagine. All you have to do is adopt the kind of lifestyle that allows that wonderful 'new you' to break out of the flabby prison that's been built around it!

The key, as always, is in the **do**, or the lifestyle that you need to adopt in order to succeed. Fad diets don't work because they are merely short-term fixes that can't be maintained over a lifetime. Fashionable exercise regimes don't work because most of them are designed to sell books and videos rather than do any real good. Only an ongoing lifestyle that is conducive to health and fitness can help you to achieve your goals – and maintain those improvements.

The lifestyle that leads to health and fitness can be boiled down to three simple habits:

- Eliminating poisons from your system

- Enjoying a healthy, balanced diet

- Exercising on a regular basis.

Let us discuss each of these in turn so that you know exactly what to do to achieve your health and fitness goals – fast and effectively.

ELIMINATE POISONS FROM YOUR SYSTEM

Despite the fact that modern society is supposed to be so health-conscious, a great many people routinely poison their physical bodies with all manner of harmful substances. Some people smoke, some drink alcohol to excess, and some even introduce illegal drugs and substances into their systems.

None of these poisons – whether they are legal or illegal – ever contributes to health and fitness. Smoking causes lung cancer and heart disease, to name just two terminal conditions. Excessive use of alcohol can damage the liver beyond repair and put a massive strain on many other internal organs. Illegal drugs can be even more immediately dangerous and often end the lives of the users without warning.

If you want to achieve health and fitness, you need to eliminate such poisons from your system, starting immediately. Quit smoking, stop drinking and don't do drugs. Of course, all of this is very easy to say in one sentence, and I understand that quitting any of these things tests your willpower to the limit. (I used to smoke 30 cigarettes a day myself, so I'm not teaching anything here that I haven't been through personally.) But believe me, if you exercise willpower, all of these things are possible. All you have to do is decide to quit and then stick to that decision, no matter how much your ego complains that it can't. It **can**, and if you stick to your guns, it will.

ADOPT A HEALTHY DIET

Your body is a finely tuned machine, and the food you put into it is the fuel that provides the energy for the machine to run. If you put poor fuel into the machine, it won't work as well as it was designed to. If you put good fuel into the machine by adopting a healthy diet, it will reward you with more energy, greater levels of health and even a more balanced emotional life.

All of this is common sense, but what exactly is a healthy diet? Well, despite what many fad-diet best-sellers would have you believe, it is quite simple to define: a healthy diet is a 50/50 balance between proteins and carbohydrates that is rich in fibre, vitamins and minerals and low in salt, saturated fat and refined sugars.

Compare this definition with what most people eat on a routine basis and you will see that they are worlds apart.

The vast majority of people here in the West consume a carb-heavy diet that is full of saturated fat as well as having high levels of salt and sugar. This kind of 'food for fun' diet plays havoc with blood sugar levels and can cause all sorts of medical problems.

Switching from a 'food for fun' diet to a 'food for fuel' diet is probably the best thing you can do for your body, apart from exercising. Get into the habit of ensuring that everything you eat benefits your body, instead of merely filling you up. Although it may be unfamiliar at first, you will find after a week or two that your tastes adjust back to their natural state, and sticking to it won't be a problem. When you get hungry, your body will start craving things like fruits, whole grains and proteins rather than a large burger and fries followed by apple pie.

Of course, this is not to say that you should never indulge in food for fun. Most experts agree that you can generally enjoy one 'fun meal' a week without sacrificing the benefits of a healthy diet, so if you want to get into the habit of having a pizza and a cream cake once a week, then there's no reason why you shouldn't. Just view such 'fun food' as the exception rather than the norm.

As well as changing what you eat, change when you eat. Most of us have been brought up to believe in the 'three square meals a day' routine, but in fact, this isn't the best way of feeding your body since it naturally leads to dips in blood sugar levels between meals. A much better eating routine is to enjoy six small meals over the course of the day, each meal being made up of some carbohydrate (an apple, some pasta, etc.), some protein (for example, a serving of tuna or chicken) and maybe a little salad to provide vitamins and minerals.

One of the main benefits of adopting this six balanced meals a day routine is that your levels of energy will remain more constant from the time you get up to the time you go to bed. And of course you will feel less hungry between meals because the meals themselves are only about three hours apart.

A word about water

Before I leave the topic of adopting a healthy diet, I would like to say a few words about water. Drinking water throughout the day is essential to developing a healthy body, since it keeps your system fully hydrated and functioning in an optimal manner. Drinks such as tea, coffee and cola, which contain caffeine, aren't generally good for the system, and tend to act as diuretics, so if you want to become as healthy as you can be, reduce your caffeine intake and increase your intake of pure water. Eight large glasses (two litres) each day is recommended as a minimum. Although this sounds like a lot, if you have one glass of water with each of your six meals, you only need to have a couple more during the day to ensure you get your full daily quota.

Benefits include clearer, younger-looking skin, better levels of all-round physical health and even improvements in mental and emotional health. Plainly, there is a lot to be said for water, but rather than just read about it, drink it and discover the benefits for yourself!

MAKE EXERCISE A HABIT

What happens when you think of exercising? Do you groan inside and wish there were an easier way to achieve your health and fitness goals? Do you imagine yourself wheezing on a treadmill, or being bored to tears doing countless sit-ups? If so, don't panic. Exercise needn't be the gruelling, joyless experience most people assume. In fact, it can be something that gives you a tremendous sense of joy and satisfaction if you go about it in the right way.

All types of physical exercise are either aerobic – 'with oxygen' – or anaerobic – 'without oxygen'. The most important form of exercise as far as health is concerned is aerobic exercise, since oxygen is vital in the process of repairing and maintaining the cells in your body. Anaerobic exercise, such as weight training, is also useful, but will not give the same benefits.

Aerobic exercise increases the amount of oxygen in the system by encouraging deeper breathing. Jogging, dancing, skipping, trampolining and swimming are all good aerobic exercises, as are sports such as squash, tennis and football, so don't think that exercise has to be boring to be effective. The fact is that if you want to play five-a-side football three times a week, then this can be just as good for you – aerobically speaking – as a session on a stationary bike or treadmill.

Aim to enjoy aerobic exercise for at least 30 minutes three times each week, and make sure that you really will enjoy it! Don't force yourself to spend hours rowing or jogging if your heart isn't in it. Instead, find a form of aerobic exercise that appeals to you and do that instead.

Whilst it is perfectly possible to exercise in your own home, you may enjoy it more if you do it in the company of other people. These could be members of your local gym or tennis club or simply neighbours who share your goal of getting fit and healthy. Exercising with other people helps you to stay motivated, keeps workout sessions fun and decreases your ability to skip a day just because you're feeling lazy.

If you haven't exercised for a while, are getting on in years or have any existing health problems, do consult your doctor before starting any exercise programme. Regular exercise is generally beneficial for everyone, but there may be some reason why you need special advice, so it makes sense to check.

As with developing any habit, exercise needs to become a part of your routine – your lifestyle – if it is to last. Check your lifestyle grid and fit in three exercise sessions – perhaps on a Monday, Wednesday and Friday – and make sure you follow them through, not just this week, but every week.

After several months of enjoying aerobic exercise three times a week, your system will be getting healthier and fitter and your metabolism will, in all likelihood, be operating more efficiently. At this stage you can take the next step, which is to add some anaerobic weight training to your life.

Thousands of people complain that they can't burn fat fast enough. They exercise aerobically three times a week and they get good results, but they can't seem to get that perfectly toned, muscular body they want. Instead, sections of fat cling to their bodies for dear life – especially on the buttocks, thighs and around the middle of their trunk.

This is because aerobic exercise, although vital for health and overall fitness, does little to strengthen and tone muscle. And the more muscle you have, the more effectively your body is able to burn excess fat. Of course, this doesn't mean that you have to become a bodybuilder to get the results you want, it just means that you need to exercise anaerobically twice a week between your aerobic sessions.

For example, if you enjoy aerobic exercise on Monday, Wednesday and Friday, you could train with weights or weight machines on Tuesdays and Thursdays. This won't give you muscles like Schwarzenegger, but most people don't want that anyway. What it will give you, and what most people do want regardless of whether they are male or female, is a sleek, toned physique that burns excess fat almost automatically.

I don't have the scope here to provide a weight training routine that would suit everyone, but your local gym will undoubtedly be able to advise you on what exercises you should do, with what weights, and how often. Men who are looking to build bigger muscles will probably be advised to use heavy weights and do three sets of eight to ten repetitions, whilst women who want to become toned rather than bulky will probably be advised to use lighter weights and do more repetitions. Your exact prescription for success in this area can only be provided by someone who is able to evaluate you in the flesh, so to speak, and help you tackle any specific problem areas you may be facing.

JOIN A GYM

I said earlier in this chapter that you don't have to join an expensive club in order to achieve the health and fitness you desire. I stand by that remark. However, I do recommend joining a more affordable gym for the following reasons:

● The gym can provide good social opportunities and give you the chance to associate with others who have also made the pursuit of health and fitness a part of their lifestyle.

● Gyms can provide far more exercise facilities than you could enjoy at home (unless you build your own) and this variety means that there is a lot less chance of you getting bored. If one piece of equipment or form of exercise starts to get boring, you can change to something else that provides enjoyment and a sense of variation.

● Visiting a gym on a regular basis doesn't have to be expensive. Unless you really want to become a member of an exclusive club, you can usually take advantage of various 'frequent user' programmes that enable you to enjoy all of the available facilities for just a small monthly fee.

Whether you decide to join a gym, exercise with friends or colleagues or even go it alone and exercise at home, it is the actual regular exercise that is important. It's not important where you do it or when you do it – just do it!

No celebrity secrets

Every week we hear of celebrities who have reinvented themselves by attaining new levels of health and fitness, and every week some newspaper or magazine promises to reveal their secrets. But the fact is, there are no celebrity secrets. Achieving any health and fitness goal is simply a matter of following a few simple rules:

● Eliminate any poisons from your system.

● Adopt a healthy, balanced diet.

● Drink lots of pure water.

● Build an aerobic base by exercising three times each week.

● Add weight training to your routine twice a week.

Make all of these habits a part of your day-to-day lifestyle and you too can reinvent yourself in any way you choose.

Career Success

When you consider that the average person will spend around 40 hours in the workplace each week for around 40 years, it isn't surprising to find that achieving career success is another goal that many of us share. I'm not talking about making money here, although that is obviously a part of what career success can provide. What I specifically mean when I refer to the goal of career success is the ability to become more effective, make work more satisfying and go as far as you are capable of going within the confines of your chosen occupation.

Of course, when you are setting goals for your own career success, you need to be far more specific than this. You need to start, as always, by defining exactly what career success means to you. Here are some examples to help you get started:

- I want to increase my personal productivity by 20 per cent within 12 months.

- I want to double my sales results within six months.

- I want to qualify for the position of supervisor within the next three years.

- I want to change to a new career within two years.

- I want to gain a formal qualification in my chosen occupation.

Obviously, this isn't a comprehensive list. There are thousands of possible career goals you could choose to set for yourself, depending on your occupation and what you want to get from your working life. Set any realistic goal you care to set. Just make sure that you attach an appropriate deadline and that the outcome is something that you can control. For example, qualifying and applying for a promotion is a goal that you can certainly achieve. Getting that promotion, on the other hand, isn't something over which you have ultimate control, and therefore the goal itself isn't valid.

Having set yourself a valid goal for career success, identify the actions you need to take and the habits you need to adopt in order to achieve this in the shortest, most effective way possible.

I have identified six things that you can do to achieve success in virtually any career, regardless of whether you are employed or self-employed. And of course, if you are currently between jobs and your career success goal is simply to find a new one, these principles will be of help to you too.

MAKE SURE YOU ARE IN THE RIGHT CAREER

The first step to achieving career success is simply to make sure that you are in the right career to begin with. All too often people get into a certain line of work for short-term reasons, then find that several years later they are still doing the same job – despite the fact that it is far removed from their original dreams of the perfect career and doesn't provide anywhere near the level of job satisfaction they had originally set out to enjoy.

Other people end up in the wrong careers simply because they themselves change, and what was once an occupation they genuinely wanted to get into now feels more like a prison of their own making.

It isn't difficult to evaluate whether or not you are already in the right career. Just answer these questions as honestly as you can:

- Did you really choose your current position or did you take it because you didn't seem to have any other option at the time?

- Do you enjoy your work?

- Does your work give you a sense of satisfaction?

- Would you be happy remaining in your current career for the rest of your working life?

- Do you feel that your current career provides all the opportunities you need for advancement?

- Does your work often provide you with a sense of fun?

- Are you already experiencing a level of success in your current career?

If you answered four or more of these questions with a 'No', then the chances are that you are in the wrong career. Succeeding in any career takes a serious commitment of time, effort and enthusiasm, but succeeding in a career that you aren't suited to is far more difficult, since you are unlikely to want to get any more involved in your occupation than you already are. If you agree with my assessment that you are in the wrong career, your first priority should be to change to another that is right for you, then return to this chapter and start applying the remaining 'steps to career success' as soon as you feel ready to do so.

If you answered 'Yes' to four or more of these questions, then the chances are that you are in the right career already. If you agree with this assessment, simply follow the remaining 'steps to career success' and make it happen!

THINK OF YOURSELF AS SELF-EMPLOYED

Regardless of whether you work for yourself or someone else, the second step to career success is to regard yourself as self-employed. Of course, this is easy to do if you do actually work for yourself, but if you work as an employee you will need to adopt a totally different attitude from the norm. Instead of seeing yourself as 'just another employee', adopt the attitude that you are really a freelance, and that you will only work in your current job for as long as you think it is beneficial.

There are several reasons why it is so important to see yourself as self-employed if you want to achieve success. For a start, **self-employed people tend to work harder than employees.** Yes, this is a generalisation, but having worked on both sides of this fence, I maintain that it is accurate in the vast majority of cases. Most employees tend to do what they need to do to remain employed and very little more. They seldom work with the same kind of intensity, commitment and passion that a self-employed individual brings to his career, because they have the security of a salary no matter how they perform.

Of course, there are exceptions to this generalisation. Some employees work extremely hard and are passionate about their careers. At the same time, some self-employed people don't give two hoots about the quality of their work and do just as little as they would for an employer. Despite these exceptions, however, the premise generally holds true.

By now you shouldn't need me to point out why hard work is so essential to achieving career success, but I'll do it anyway to save you having to refer back to Part I. **Hard work is essential because results follow action.** Take only a little action by performing in a typically mediocre 'employee' fashion and you will only get typically mediocre 'employee' kinds of success. Take massive action by working hard, day in and day out, with intensity and passion, and you will achieve far greater levels of success.

The second reason is that **self-employed people tend to be more flexible** than employees. Employees tend to like the idea of security and dislike change. They like to get into a routine (or should I say a rut?) and keep things as predictable as possible. Self-employed people can't afford to do that. The business world is constantly changing and evolving, and if a self-employed individual is to succeed over the long term he has to learn early on that flexibility is essential. He needs to move with the times, adjust his supply to meet fluctuating market demand and be prepared to make any changes that become necessary in order to evolve and remain valuable in an ever-changing world.

By viewing yourself as self-employed, even if you work for someone else, this flexible attitude will enable you to succeed when everyone else is being made redundant. For example, if your company starts replacing people with computers, you will either learn to become one of the few people who can operate those computers, or start looking for a new position immediately. Most of the people around you, however, will spend their time complaining to the union and moaning that things were fine just the way they used to be. These people won't start looking for a new position or try to become computer literate until it's too late – if they get around to it at all.

In other words, flexibility enables you to adapt to any changes in your working environment and conditions whilst others freeze like rabbits caught by the headlights of a car. If your job stops working for you, you must be flexible and get a different one. If the company you work for develops a new way of operating, you must embrace that change and set out to master the new approach. You must be totally flexible, and that flexibility will ensure your long-term success, no matter how things change around you.

The third main reason why it is essential for you to see yourself as being self-employed is because **self-employed people know their true value**. Employees often don't. Instead, they assume that they are worth what they are currently being paid, and this is a big mistake.

If you are currently on a salary of £20,000 per year, this doesn't mean that you are really worth £20,000. It could be that you work with great efficiency and skill, and add perhaps a quarter of a million pounds-worth of value to your company. In this case, your true value is much more than £20,000. Even if you define your value as just 20 per cent of the value you generate, you are worth £50,000 a year.

Of course, someone else in a £20,000-a-year position could be coasting along, contributing a minimum of effort and adding only £80,000 of value to his company. In this case, using 20 per cent of created value as a salary guide, the employee is worth only £16,000.

Self-employed people tend to be very good at assessing their true value. They know what they can do and what the market rate is for working on a certain project. With this accurate data in mind, they only take on projects that will reward them according to their true value. If a lawyer is worth £100 an hour, he will charge £100 an hour. Try to hire him for £20 an hour and the chances are that he won't want to know.

This is the kind of mindset that you must adopt towards your career. Let's say that you are earning £20,000 a year for creating £125,000-worth of value for your company. By viewing yourself as self-employed, you should immediately approach your employer and point this out to him. Ask for the extra £5,000 that you know you are worth. If necessary, find out what other people who create similar levels of value are earning in your industry. If they are earning more than you, use this fact to back up your case.

You should never forget that when you are working – whether it is for a client if you are self-employed or for your boss if you are an employee – you are actually selling your life in eight-hour segments. If you are to be truly happy in your career, you need to ensure that the deal is worthwhile. Working an eight-hour day for £100 is probably not too bad a deal, but working the same eight-hour day for £16... well, you could earn that much just mowing lawns in the evening, so why accept £16 for a whole day? You're worth more than that.

Celebrities are ideal examples of people who know their true value and insist on being paid accordingly. Maybe you think that paying an actor $20 million to appear in a movie is extravagant, but if the actor's involvement generates $100 million or more in profits, I'd say that the studio is getting a fair deal.

By viewing yourself as self-employed, you will start to take a closer look at what you are being paid compared with the amount of value you create for your boss or client. If you can't get paid what you are truly worth, go elsewhere. On the other hand, if you get paid more than you feel you are truly worth, aim to increase your value fast before someone else finds out!

DO MORE THAN YOU ARE PAID TO DO

Having just talked about making sure that you get paid according to your true value, I am now going to suggest that a major step to career success is to do more than you are paid to do.

This is because by doing more than you are paid to do, you will get the personal satisfaction of being a contributor. This step isn't about money, it's about feeling fulfilled in your work. It's not about allowing yourself to be exploited by a mean employer, it's about going the extra mile and doing something for the sake of doing it, rather than just because you are getting paid to do it.

If your work is nothing more than a means of earning money, you will never feel really satisfied in your career. Yes, you might make a lot of money, receive promotions and enjoy all manner of material benefits, but you won't ever know the joy of actually contributing value simply for the sake of giving.

I know a man who has a small window-cleaning business. He knows the true value of his work and sets his fees accordingly, but every time he does his rounds he cleans the windows of several homes for free. He does this because the people who live in these particular homes can't afford for him to clean their windows regularly, so he just provides his valuable service for the sake of giving. And what is more, he makes a point of cleaning those 'free' windows just as well as he does for all his paying clients. That way he knows he's actually giving away something that is genuinely worth paying for.

Over the years this man has probably missed out on several thousand pounds-worth of business by taking the time to clean the windows of these no-fee homes, but what he has gained in terms of personal satisfaction, fulfilment and happiness could never be bought at any price. He has become good friends with many of these 'special clients' and even when some of their circumstances change so that they can afford to pay him, he refuses to accept their offers. 'I don't clean your windows for money,' he tells them, 'I clean them for you.'

If you think this story is a little saccharin, then you obviously need to start doing more than you are paid to do. Adopt the habit of doing at least one thing each day that is above and beyond the call of duty. Don't do it because you think your boss will notice and reward you. Don't do it because you want to close a particular sale. Don't do it because you think such selflessness will make you look good in front of your colleagues. Just do it for the sake of doing it, and for the incredible sense of personal fulfilment and satisfaction that such actions bring.

BE EFFECTIVE IN YOUR WORK

The fourth step towards career success is to learn to be effective. When you assessed your true value earlier in this chapter, you did so based on the amount of value you create for your boss or clients at the present time. By becoming more effective, you will find that you can increase your true value even more and progress even further towards the goal you have set for yourself.

My definition of being effective is simple: being effective is doing the things that genuinely get results.

To become more effective in your work, spend some time thinking about what the real aim of your job is, then make sure that you spend most of your time doing things that help you to achieve that aim rather than wasting it on associated trivialities.

For example, some years ago I met a life insurance salesman who was struggling to meet his targets. Other people in his office were doing well, so it wasn't a case of there being poor market conditions. Wanting to get to the core of his problem, I observed him for a few days and found that he spent 80 per cent of his time completing and filing paperwork and only 20 per cent of his time actually trying to sell insurance policies. His more successful colleagues, by comparison, spent 80 per cent of their time selling policies and only 20 per cent on paperwork.

I asked him why he did things this way and he said that the other guys relied on the administrative staff to do most of their paperwork. He went on to explain that he didn't want to do that, because he didn't trust them to do it as well as he could.

I pointed out that if the paperwork wasn't filed properly, the world wouldn't come to an end. And by getting the admin staff to handle the majority of his paperwork, he could afford to spend a full 80 per cent of his time on doing what was most important – selling life insurance policies.

He agreed to adopt this approach in an effort to be more effective in his work. Of course, the administration staff did a fine job at completing and filing his paperwork, and the salesman soon started meeting – and then exceeding – his monthly sales targets.

The point here is that if you want to succeed in your career, you need to focus on doing things that matter, rather than doing things that really don't have much importance. Review the main aim of your job and then make sure that you spend most of your time pursuing that aim. Don't stand chatting by the coffee machine for 20 minutes at a time. Don't take extended lunch hours. Don't make personal phone calls from the office. Just do your job and get results. Be more effective.

BECOME A GOOD COMMUNICATOR

The people who advance the fastest in their careers are invariably good communicators. They know how to get their point across to others. They know how to listen to what other people have to say. They make people feel at ease with themselves and therefore excel in their ability to negotiate with others and diffuse potentially difficult interpersonal situations.

If you want to achieve career success, you too need to learn to become a good communicator. It is impossible to become successful without involving and dealing with other people, so make your life easier by developing the skills you need to communicate in the best, most effective way possible.

I don't have the space here for a detailed discussion of good communication skills, so I strongly recommend that you take action on your own: take a course of study, read a book on successful communication or do whatever else is required, but make becoming a good communicator a priority. To start you off, see the points on page 118.

GET A LIFE

The sixth and last step to career success is to get a life. Achieving success in your career is not the be-all and end-all of your existence. Your aim here is not to become a workaholic with a one-track mind, but to achieve career success so that other parts of your life can benefit too.

By all means, work hard. Work six days a week if you want to. But set aside the seventh day, and other time if possible, to devote to other things. Spend time with your family and friends. Enjoy a rewarding hobby. Go and have a meal in a nice restaurant. Whatever you do in these moments, put thoughts of your career on hold. Detach yourself from it until it is time to start work again.

It may sound a little paradoxical, but putting aside your career and enjoying other areas of your life actually helps you to succeed in your career. There are three reasons why this is so.

- You will dramatically reduce the chances of 'burn-out', which, in extreme cases, could end your career altogether.

- You will actually feel more refreshed when you do eventually get back to work. This renewed energy will enable you to be even more effective – and therefore successful – in your chosen occupation.

- You will remain aware that your job is not your identity to any extent. Your career serves only two purposes: to provide you with an income and to provide you with opportunities to make a contribution to society whilst achieving a sense of personal fulfilment.

Now that we have discussed the six steps to career success, go out and act on all that you have learned. Set yourself a personal career goal that you can realistically achieve, then apply the six steps in conjunction with all you learned in Part I of this book and get to work. **Be** the person you need to be, **do** the things you need to do and **have** the successful career you want to have.

Successful Relationships

Successful relationships are the life-blood of a satisfying life. They provide companionship, love, sex, friendship and a myriad of other positive benefits that make our lives richer, happier and more fulfilling.

Unfortunately many people don't enjoy successful relationships simply because they have never set out to make them successful. The vast majority allow their relationships to develop on their own, in any direction that fate happens to take them, and all too often this leads to relationships that are routine, stagnant and far from satisfying. Indeed, when left untended, a very large number of relationships break down altogether.

If you want to enjoy all the benefits of having successful relationships, you need to break away from this apathy and actually work on making them successful. Of course, we've all heard that we need to put effort into our relationships in order to make them work, but how many people actually do invest the effort? Fewer than we'd like to believe, I'm prepared to bet.

Because relationships by their very nature involve other people, it is never possible to be in total control of what happens to them or to dictate with certainty how they will develop over the weeks, months and years. However, the way that you behave in a relationship has a major impact on the way it is likely to develop, and your own actions are certainly under your control. The goal of achieving more successful relationships is therefore perfectly valid as long as you realise that you aren't the only one responsible for the way they work out. As the saying goes, it takes two to tango, and it takes at least that number to make a relationship as good as it can be.

In this chapter we will discuss the actions and habits you need to incorporate into your lifestyle in order to achieve more success in your personal relationships with friends, partners and colleagues. (Family relationships – those you have with parents, children, cousins, aunts, uncles, etc. – can be a lot more complex than one-to-one relationships, so we shall deal with them on their own terms in Chapter 9.)

The actions and habits that you need to take and adopt can be presented as 'rules' and divided into three main categories:

- **Generic rules,** which apply to all relationships

- **Platonic rules,** which apply specifically to non-sexual and non-romantic relationships

- **Intimate rules,** which apply specifically to relationships that involve an element of sex and/or romance

Many relationships move from one category to another as they develop. For example, we might start out having a generic relationship with a work colleague and gradually become close friends, in which case the platonic rules come into play. If the relationship progresses even further into one that includes sexual and/or romantic elements, the intimate rules would also apply.

Don't feel bound by these categories. If you have relationships that are midway between platonic and intimate, just apply whichever rules you feel are more appropriate. This book isn't about dictating what you should and shouldn't do. It's simply about ensuring that you know what actions and habits can be applied to achieve certain goals. Whether you take those actions and apply those habits is entirely up to you.

GENERIC RULES

There are four generic rules that I have identified. These can be used to help virtually any relationship to improve and become more satisfying – for everyone involved.

Love yourself

The first rule of all successful relationships is to love yourself. This might sound incredibly selfish, but I'm not talking about vanity here. I'm talking about treating yourself with the respect, care and attention you deserve. Unless you do this, you can't really expect others to respect you, care about you or give you any attention.

A big mistake that vast numbers of individuals make is to look to others for a sense of validation that they are worth something. You don't need that kind of external validation. You are infinitely valuable with or without the approval of others. You may have done things or said things in your life that you regret, but that doesn't mean that you are worth less than anyone else. It simply means that you are human and therefore have a few imperfections.

Learn to accept yourself, warts and all, and instead of beating yourself up about the flaws you recognise within yourself, just decide to work on becoming all that you are capable of becoming. We all have our good points, and if you focus on these, nurturing and encouraging them, the flaws will fade into the background almost automatically.

There are many ways to love yourself, but they all boil down to the same thing: giving yourself personal time and attention. Consider the following ideas as starting points.

- **Take care of your body.** Go to the gym. Eat a healthy diet. Give up smoking. Take a holiday and relax. Have a manicure, pedicure or massage. Whatever you do, treat your body with the respect and care it deserves.

- **Give yourself time out.** We often spend so much time with other people that we forget who we really are. Aim to spend at least half an hour each day on your own so that you can rediscover yourself and start meeting more of your own needs.

- **Do something for fun.** Get involved in a hobby or interest that you have always wanted to take part in. Learn to paraglide, scuba dive, speak French, paint with oils, play the electric guitar or whatever else takes your fancy. Don't feel guilty about doing something purely for your own pleasure. You deserve it!

- **Be complete within yourself.** Don't view relationships of any kind as being essential to your existence. They aren't. Successful relationships can help to make your life richer and more satisfying, but this doesn't mean that you can't be happy and satisfied to a great extent without the input of other people. The aim of building relationships is to improve the satisfaction and fulfilment you already have in your life, not to provide these things from scratch.

Once you start learning to love yourself, something remarkable will happen. You will become more confident, other people will find you more interesting and as a result of both these things, your relationships with everyone around you will start improving.

Be externally focused

Once you have learned to love yourself, there will be no need for you to spend all of your time trying to get others to validate your worth. Instead, you will be able to focus on people other than yourself. Not only will this make other people feel special, but it will also help you to become a genuinely rounded and caring person, rather than someone who goes to extremes of introspection.

We all know people who, neglecting the first rule of loving themselves, see relationships only as vehicles for receiving the praise, encouragement, love and acceptance that we all need and want. The problem with looking for these things solely from other people is that it makes such people appear needy, or selfish and self-centred. They spend hours talking about themselves and when the topic of conversation finally turns to someone else, they get restless and quickly move on to the next available sounding board.

This rule and the previous one therefore work most effectively in tandem. Love yourself, then go out and put other people first. Be externally focused and the people you meet will think you're amazing.

Become a good communicator

We talked about communication skills in the previous chapter, but they also play a pivotal role in determining whether or not we achieve successful, satisfying relationships. The number one reason for people having poor relationships is that one, or both, of the parties haven't learned how to communicate effectively.

As I said in the previous chapter, I suggest that you study communication skills more fully. Take a class, attend a seminar or simply read a book that is specifically geared towards improving your communication skills within the context of relationships. Educate yourself in this way and your relationships will improve beyond all recognition.

To get you started, here are a few basic communication guidelines that you might want to start using immediately:

- **Always think before you speak.** Often it's the little things that 'slip out' that cause the most trouble in relationships. Think before you say anything, and if you can't say something positive, don't say anything. Even if you are invited to offer criticism or comments, you should only ever do so in a positive, encouraging way.

- **Make lots of eye contact and smile.** These two visual habits can transform the quality of your relationships more than you would ever believe. These signals tell people that you are open and friendly, and will instantly help to put other people at ease.

- **Listen rather than speaking.** You were born with two ears and one mouth. Use these physical attributes in the same proportion and you will automatically become a more effective communicator. Rather than jumping in time after time to make your own point in a conversation, listen to the other point of view without bias. You just might find that it makes sense.

- **Agree to disagree.** Don't think that in order to have great relationships, everyone has to agree all of the time. They don't, and expecting everyone to agree with your point of view will do a lot more harm than good. Accept the fact that we all perceive the world in slightly different ways. You are not always right and the people you speak to are not always wrong. Agree to disagree on certain topics and don't make a disagreement on one or two points a personal issue.

Don't try to force friendships

Achieving success in your relationships doesn't mean that everyone you meet will become your new best friend. The fact is that none of us gets on equally well with everyone else, and expecting such an unrealistic outcome is only setting yourself up for disappointment.

Because of your background, beliefs, life experiences, personality, attitudes and a host of other factors, you will find that you gel more naturally with some people and less naturally with others. Accept this. If you meet someone who you don't immediately 'click' with, be friendly, polite and courteous, but don't waste time trying to force this person to become your best friend. Instead, leave them be. You can't be the best of friends with everyone.

PLATONIC RULES

Under the category of platonic rules I have defined two simple rules that, when used in conjunction with the generic rules already discussed, can help to make your close friendships more successful.

Make time for the relationship

The first platonic rule is that you must make time for your close friendships. Don't think that you can enjoy successful, solid friendships without actually spending some time together. This needn't be a lot of time – there is no need for you and your friends to live in each other's pockets – but you should schedule regular periods when you can enjoy each other's company. Perhaps you'd like to spend a couple of hours together at the gym each week, or maybe enjoy a night out twice a month or so. Whatever type of activity you feel is most suited to you both, make time to do something together at least every other week.

If you don't do this, or if you allow other, newer relationships to 'steal' time from your existing friendships, you will find that the friendships gradually weaken in strength, and often dissolve to the point where you are virtual strangers. This happens a lot when two single friends each find a romantic partner and work on these romantic relationships to the neglect of all else. Their original friendship loses its strength and before long it turns into something only slightly more than an acquaintance.

This is a great shame, because our close platonic friendships can be a rich source of support, stability and perspective in our lives. Of course, there is nothing wrong with people moving on in life and permitting their close friendships to take a back seat every now and again, but allowing them to lose all of their original meaning is a terrible waste.

The bottom line is that if you want your close platonic friendships to succeed, your first priority must be to make time for them, not just every once in a while, but on a regular basis.

Don't judge

If there is one thing that can wreck a perfectly good friendship, it is when either party starts to judge the other's behaviour, actions or speech.

Of course, this doesn't mean that you have to agree with or even condone what your friends do. There might be times when one of your close friends does something that you consider to be morally wrong. In such a case you should feel free to air this opinion, but don't judge your friend for having a different one.

This principle of not judging others is often a difficult one to live by. You can make it a little easier by understanding that all human beings do what they think is best in virtually all situations, and then examine the situation from your friend's point of view. Try to understand why they did whatever it was they did; look beyond the action to the motivation behind that action and in the vast majority of cases your desire to judge will disappear.

If you can get into the habit of being non-judgmental, your friendships will be closer and more open than they could ever be otherwise. Your friends won't feel the need to mask themselves in your presence for fear of your opinion. Instead, you can enjoy relationships of total honesty and even if you don't approve of some of the things your friends do, they will know that you accept them regardless.

INTIMATE RULES

The third and final category of rules applies to intimate relationships – those that involve an element of romantic love or sexuality. Once again, all of the previous rules that we have discussed apply equally to intimate relationships, but here we add three more.

Remain an individual

One of the most important things you can do in any intimate relationship is retain your own identity and remain an individual. This sounds obvious, but many people don't do it. Instead, they begin to identify themselves as **being** the relationship instead of as an individual who simply enjoys the relationship. If this case of 'false identity' continues, then eventually the individual won't be able to think outside the context of a relationship. If the relationship then comes to an end, for whatever reason, this person who has allowed it to become their very identity will, in all probability, find themselves plunged into a major emotional and psychological crisis.

No matter how much you love or care for someone, you should remind yourself often that you are still an individual. You are not someone else's 'other half', you are complete in yourself.

If you work hard to make sure that you retain your identity as an individual, you will find that your relationship becomes much healthier as a result. You and your partner will be less likely to take each other for granted. You will have more respect for one another. And you will both find it a lot easier to apply the next rule of intimate relationships.

Give each other some freedom

Having an intimate relationship that is successful and fulfilling doesn't mean that you have to suffocate each other. It is just as important to allow each other freedom as it is to spend quality time together.

Lots of people fail to do this. I know one couple who haven't spent more than an afternoon apart in over ten years. They work together, live together, eat together and sleep together. They see this as a display of immense commitment. I see it as a potentially major relationship problem in the making, because we all need a certain amount of freedom to be our own person, follow our own interests and be selfish every now and again.

Before you misunderstand me, I'm not condoning so-called 'open relationships' that give both partners the freedom to sleep with other people whenever they choose. In my opinion – and you are free to disagree with me if you wish – this is taking the principle of freedom in intimate relationships a little too far.

What I am talking about here is giving each other the freedom to grow as individuals, to discover yourselves more fully, to explore aspects of life that you have always wanted to explore.

You can't do this unless you give and receive a certain amount of freedom. Be committed to each other, certainly. Live together, by all means. But don't think that just because you're in an intimate relationship, you have to spend every spare moment together, or that you have to hold the same points of view without ever disagreeing.

Give each other freedom by making sure that you allow each other the time and space needed to develop as individuals. Do this and you will find that the relationship itself becomes stronger and better developed.

Vary the game

Monotony can kill virtually any relationship if you allow it to. Like weeds that take over a garden, monotonous routines, habits and ruts can all make your relationship lose its appeal, and the grass in other gardens will suddenly seem an awful lot greener.

The percentage of relationships that end either directly or indirectly because of boredom and monotony is considerable. Yet there is no universal law that states that intimate relationships have to get boring and stale. You can keep virtually any relationship fresh and alive if you get into the habit of varying the game every now and them.

Varying the game simply means doing things differently and breaking up dull routines by introducing new, fresh alternatives. Perhaps you and your partner always go to the same place when you have a night out? In this case, you could vary the game by going somewhere you've never been before. Other ways of varying different aspects of 'the game' could include:

- Making a spontaneous decision to go away for the weekend.

- Going out to eat instead of staying at home.

- Making love somewhere other than in the bedroom.

- Turning off the television and playing a game together.

- Introducing more exotic foods into your cooking.

- Trying new sexual positions or techniques.

- Starting new shared hobbies and interests.

- Joining new clubs and meeting new friends.

Obviously, there are an infinite number of ways in that you could change your particular 'game', so feel free to be original. Identify any dull routines that have managed to establish themselves in your relationship and come up with several ways to break them and introduce more variety into your lives at the same time.

This is a simple habit to adopt, but doing so will ensure that your intimate relationship never gets to that dangerous point where predictability and routine take over. Keep your partner on their toes (and encourage them to keep you on yours!) and you will both enjoy a much more spontaneous, living kind of relationship.

When applying any of what I have said in this chapter to your relationships, don't feel bound by the categories that I have defined here. Study the rules I have presented and apply them in whatever manner seems most appropriate to you and your situation. Relationships come in all shapes and sizes, so adapt the principles you have learned here to suit. Just remember, no relationship will ever look after itself. You need to invest time and effort into making your relationships as successful, satisfying and fulfilling as they can be.

Emotional Success

Generally speaking, emotional success isn't something that you hear many people talking about achieving. You hear plenty about people wanting to achieve financial success and career success, but only rarely does someone speak of achieving emotional success. This is a great pity, for achieving emotional success can have just as big an impact on our lives as achieving more money or a better career – if not even bigger.

Emotional success can be defined as the ability to control your emotions instead of having them control you. Unfortunately, allowing emotions to control us is all too common a habit. Consider the following examples.

- A man gets caught in a traffic-jam. Already feeling stressed about problems he is having at work and in his personal relationship with his wife, he suddenly snaps, suffering an attack of road rage. He gets out of the car and starts assaulting the driver in front, either verbally or perhaps even physically.

- A woman is getting ready for a dinner party. Already three people have had to cancel, and now the roast is burnt to a cinder because the oven thermostat has blown. She runs out of the kitchen in tears.

Have you ever wondered why sometimes even the smallest things can have a dramatic effect on your emotions? Have you ever asked yourself why you react to things in the way that you do? Have you ever snapped at your children, associates or partner and then immediately regretted it?

The problem in all of these scenarios is that we tend to react to situations as if we were on some kind of automatic pilot. Only later, when we, 'come to our senses' do we analyse what happened and realise that we allowed our emotions to get out of control once again.

Wouldn't it be nice if we could actually remain in control of our emotions all of the time? Wouldn't it be good if we could assess a situation and then deliberately choose the most appropriate emotion to respond with? This might sound like a far-fetched idea, but it is in fact perfectly possible, and the actions you need to take to achieve such a goal of emotional success are far simpler than you probably think they are.

THE BODY/MIND CONNECTION

The body and the mind are inextricably linked. The posture and movement of the physical body affect the emotions we experience, and the emotions we experience affect the posture and movement of the physical body. Thus the body/mind connection can be likened to a 'loop' that runs largely on auto-pilot. By deliberately breaking this loop and changing the way in which the physical body is being used, the loop can be used to generate a more appropriate emotional response.

Consider a man who is mildly depressed, for example. This emotional state will affect his body in a number of ways. His shoulders will slump, his facial muscles will slacken and his head will droop a little. His breathing will be shallow, and his eyes will tend to look down towards the floor. This is the physical body's way of expressing the emotion of mild 'depression'.

To pull himself out of this depressed state, all this man needs to do is deliberately interrupt the body/mind loop by radically altering his body posture. If he stands up straight, puts a big smile on his face, breaths deeply, holds his head high and looks up instead of down, the emotion of mild depression will begin to disappear.

Understanding this body/mind connection can provide you with a real breakthrough in achieving emotional success, because all you have to do to experience any emotion is define the 'formula' of physical postures and actions that go along with that emotion, then deliberately move your body into that state. The body/mind connection will do the rest and will start generating the emotion of its own accord.

Emotion formulae

Here are three formulae that you can use deliberately to create more confidence, tranquillity or excitement whenever you need to.

Formula 1: For confidence

- Stand tall, with your head high.
- Lift up your chin.
- Put your shoulders back.
- Clench your fists.
- Smile big and broad.
- Take ten powerful, deep breaths.

Formula 2: For tranquillity

- Sit on a chair or on the floor, with your back straight.

- Close your eyes and rest your hands in your lap.

- Smile gently (inwardly, if you prefer).

- Take ten slow, deep breaths.

- Repeat the word 'Peace' to yourself – aloud or silently – until you achieve the desired state of tranquillity.

Formula 3: For excitement

- Stand tall.

- Look up.

- Clench your fists and throw your arms high into the air, as if you were celebrating a goal you have just scored in a World Cup match.

- Open your eyes wide and smile as wide as you can.

- Jump up and down on the spot, saying 'Yes, yes, yes!'

- Continue doing this for 30 to 60 seconds, until you feel the desired sense of excitement.

As you can see, these formulae are very simple. All they consist of is a particular body posture and/or movement, facial expression and rate of breathing. There is nothing magical about any of them. In fact you can easily create your own formulae for emotions by thinking of any emotion you want and then noting three things:

- How you move your body when experiencing this emotion.

- How you smile or use your facial muscles when experiencing this emotion.

- How you breathe when experiencing this emotion.

Armed with this information, all you need to do to spark off this emotion is move your body, adjust your facial muscles and breathe accordingly. The body/mind connection will do the rest and start generating the desired emotion in an instant.

INTERNAL REPRESENTATION

The second approach to creating any emotion you want to experience is to use the power of music to adjust the way in which you internally represent the reality you experience. Music has always been used to produce changes in emotion and even altered states of consciousness in some cultures, and you can put this proven tool to work in your own life.

Studies have been done to find out how much music affects our emotions and the results have been quite remarkable. People who listen to various types of music in their cars were assessed and the following conclusions were made:

● Slow, gentle music such as classical or 'new age' peace music helps to generate emotions of calmness, tranquillity and centredness.

● Middle-of-the-road, easy-listening 'lounge' music generates emotions of happiness, contentment and general enjoyment of life.

● Popular music with a regular, rapid beat generates emotions of confidence and happiness.

● Heavy rock music and dance music with a fast beat generate emotions of excitement and sometimes aggression.

This list is not exhaustive of course, there are many other types of music and different reactions to them.

All you have to do is choose an emotion you want to feel more often, and then identify the type of music that will promote this feeling and listen to it whenever you want to.

For example, maybe you would like to feel confident and successful as you drive to work each morning. The first step you would take would be to decide what kinds of songs or tunes make you feel confident and successful when you listen to them. Then you would record these songs on to a tape, CD or MP3 device until you have at least an hour of music. Once that is done you can simply listen to this 'power album' every morning in your car and the desired emotion will follow almost automatically.

If you are really sincere about achieving emotional success, then you could create a separate power album for a number of different emotions, such as tranquillity, joy, confidence, and so on. This will create a kind of library of emotions that you can pick and choose from at will. For example, you could listen to pop music in your car on the way to work to get 'psyched up' and then listen to easy-listening or classical music on your drive home to calm down ready for a relaxing evening.

Taking control of your emotions gets a lot easier the more you practise it. From now on you need never feel overwhelmed by stress, depression, helplessness, nervousness or any other negative emotion. By adopting the habits of using your body/mind connection and power albums deliberately to generate the emotions you most want to experience, your achievement of emotional success is virtually guaranteed.

Start right now. Choose one emotion that you would like to experience on a regular basis and create your own appropriate power album. Then master the body/mind formulae contained in this chapter (or create your own as instructed) and use them whenever necessary to achieve the state of mind you require.

Achieving emotional success really is as simple as that!

A Successful Family Life

*T*he aim of this chapter is to examine the kind of actions and habits that need to be taken and adopted in order for you to help nurture a healthy family unit, or what I refer to simply as 'family success'.

There so many different kinds of families that defining what makes them successful in a broad manner is virtually impossible. For example, here are two very common definitions of a successful family:

- A successful family is one where everyone supports and relies on each other.

- A successful family is one where each member grows up to be completely independent.

These two definitions are perfectly valid, but not at all the same. What might represent 'success' to one person could indicate failure to the other, and vice versa.

For the purposes of this chapter, I will not attempt to define what success means. Instead, I will assume that there are certain traits that are common to all successful families, no matter how the term is defined, and discuss the actions and habits that can be taken and adopted so that each of these traits can be encouraged as much as possible.

PLANNED FAMILY TIME

Successful families get together on a regular basis, and that doesn't mean just once a year at Christmas. If you don't get together with your immediate family at least once a week, and with your extended family at least three times each year, there is obviously plenty of room for improvement.

Get into the habit of planning family time – not just so that you know exactly when you will all be able to get together, but also so that you will be able to make that time as interesting and enjoyable as you can for everyone.

The purpose of the family spending time together is not primarily to discuss shopping lists or washing-up rotas, but simply to enjoy each other's company on a regular basis. One week you might plan a day at the zoo. Another week you might plan a picnic, or building a den for the children in the garden. The actual 'event' that you plan your time around is not particularly important. All that matters is that you do in fact spend time enjoyably in each other's company. As the saying goes, families that play together, stay together.

A HARMONIOUS ENVIRONMENT

The second thing you can do to promote a strong, healthy family is to make the family home as comfortable and harmonious as possible. The more each member of your family feels able to relax and unwind at home, the less they will feel the need to 'escape' to some other place. Of course, this doesn't mean that you should expect the family to get together each and every day without each member pursuing his or her own interests. What it does mean is that even as members of the family go about their lives, a harmonious environment will encourage them to pause and smile to each other on the way.

What the term 'harmonious environment' specifically means to you is of course a personal matter, but generally it means an environment where every member of your household feels content, secure and happy to spend time.

Many modern homes revolve around the television, so it is no surprise that many people find it difficult to communicate with each other. Consider moving furniture so that conversation and other activities are given more focus than television. Replace the TV guide on the coffee table with a board game or two – or even a video games console. Two people interacting with a video game is a lot healthier than them simply sitting down to watch four hours of television without speaking.

There are never any hard and fast rules about creating an environment that your particular family finds to be harmonious. Some families need Zen-style minimalist layout and décor to feel relaxed and peaceful. Others need lots of activities to encourage interaction. You know your family better than anyone else, so arrange your environment in such a way that everyone will enjoy spending time together. If you all love music, make that the focal point of your main lounge area. If you are all passionate about exercise, turning the basement into a home gym could be all it takes to get everyone interacting in the same room.

Whatever you do to make your home more harmonious, you will know that you have succeeded when your family gathers informally to chat, laugh and play instead of simply treating the home as a convenient terminal that they merely pass through on their way to somewhere else.

HONEST COMMUNICATION

As I have already said, the ability to communicate well plays a major role in the achievement of this 'healthy family' goal. Make sure that everyone in the family is free to express themselves and that each person's opinion is listened to and acknowledged. Nine out of ten inter-family arguments and disagreements are caused by a lack of proper communication, so taking the action of making good communication a priority could be a major step towards overall success in this area.

If a family member ever raises a problem or grievance, ensure that something is done about it. Don't fall into the trap of listening to people but then continuing to act as before, regardless of what has been said. If a problem is aired, help to provide a solution. Involve other members of the family as appropriate and work through any difficulties together. You will find that by taking this approach, problems can provide great opportunities for the family to grow even stronger as you all work together to solve them.

A good starting-point for honest communication could be to share with your family all that you have learned in this book. Talk about your desire to create a more harmonious family environment and to spend more time together doing fun things. Ask for input from the other members of your family. What do they want from the family? How do they think the family could be strengthened and the home made more conducive to healthy family interaction? By getting everyone involved, the very act of trying to make the family relationships stronger could strengthen them automatically.

Freedom, tolerance and respect

You can choose your friends, but you can't choose your family members. This is a trite old saying, but the truth it conveys is nevertheless valuable. The fact is that just because several people belong to the same family, and even live under the same roof, this doesn't mean that they will always share the same views and opinions. In fact, in many cases their opinions and beliefs will be contradictory. This needn't cause a problem as long as everyone in the family gives everyone else personal freedom and practises tolerance and respect for one another.

To a great extent, all of this can be done simply by accepting people as they are and realising that if everyone were exactly the same, the world would be a very dull place indeed. The straight father should accept his gay son without reservation. The son, an enthusiastic carnivore, should respect the vegetarian views of his sister. Within a strong and healthy family, it shouldn't matter who is straight or gay, vegetarian or carnivore, Buddhist or Christian. It certainly shouldn't matter that not all members of the family agree on musical tastes, political allegiances or fashion preferences.

A strong, healthy family is not one in which everyone agrees. Anyone can remain at peace when they are in agreement with another. The strong and healthy family is one that doesn't allow trivial or even major differences in opinion to jeopardise their relationships, and this can only be achieved if everyone gives each other freedom and becomes more tolerant and respectful.

These four main traits of a successful family are all it takes to achieve strength in your family relationships. Spend time together, create a harmonious environment, communicate honestly and practise freedom, tolerance and respect. If you adopt these traits, then even though the dynamic of family relationships can sometimes be incredibly complex, you will achieve your goal.

Spiritual Fulfilment

There are millions of people who have achieved success in their finances, relationships, health, careers, emotional lives and even in their families, but who still don't feel as though they have the level of personal fulfilment they originally wanted. This is because a genuine, all-encompassing sense of fulfilment doesn't come from having more money, a great body or even a wildly adventurous sex life. True peace of mind and fulfilment can only come when we aim to develop our spiritual lives.

I should state here and now that I am in no way an evangelist and I do not want to push religion on anyone. As far as I am concerned, all religions serve basically the same purpose, which is to provide the seeker with a sense of connection to the divine. If you already follow a spiritual path, be it Christianity, Buddhism, Paganism, Shamanism, Hinduism, Eckankar, Scientology or any other, then as long as it is providing you with a sense of spiritual fulfilment you should continue on the path you have chosen.

For those of you who haven't yet pursued spiritual fulfilment in any meaningful way, and don't particularly want to follow a traditional religious path, I would like to provide you with three spiritual practices that you can introduce into your life. They will help you to experience this sense of 'divine connection' without having to go to a temple or church or adopt any formal religious path. Study each idea as it is presented, and if it appeals to you, try including it in your life for a few months. Then, if you find that you benefit from having done so, retain the practice.

MEDITATE DAILY

Meditation is one of the world's oldest spiritual disciplines, yet it is still the most popular, and for good reason. Meditation is scientifically proven to calm the body as well as the mind. When practised regularly, it helps to reduce stress levels, lower blood pressure and even assist in overcoming physical addictions.

From the spiritual point of view, meditation can open us up to a whole new 'interior world' and give us very real sense of connection with the divine aspect of the universe, whatever the word 'divine' means to you. This being the case, some people view meditation practice as the real 'key discipline' to reaching virtually any desired level of spiritual fulfilment.

Below I explain how to start a simple daily meditation practice. When you have tried this, you can go on to explore other forms of the discipline in whatever way appeals to you – either by reading books on the subject or by attending local meditation classes on a regular basis.

To begin, find a quiet place where you will not be disturbed. Sit on the floor, on a cushion or in a chair and close your eyes. Take a few deep breaths and allow your body to relax. Keep your spine as straight as you can and allow your hands to rest in your lap or on your knees.

Now focus your entire attention on your breathing. 'Watch' the breath as it enters your nostrils on every inhalation, then as it leaves on every exhalation. If you wish, you can count the breaths, counting 'one' for the inhalation, 'two' for the exhalation, 'three' for the next inhalation, and so on, starting all over again when the count reaches ten.

Continue doing this for around 20 to 30 minutes, and aim to keep your focus on your breathing for the entire duration. This ability comes with practice, and at first you will probably find it quite difficult to keep your mind focused. Instead, other thoughts might creep into your mind. You might suddenly remember a deadline you have to meet, a bill you need to pay or a meal you need to take out of the freezer. Whatever distractions occur, push them aside and return your attention to your breathing.

When you end your meditation session, don't simply jump up and get back to the business of living. Take a few slow, deep breaths, open your eyes slowly and allow the peace of the meditation to stay with you as you gently return to your normal duties.

The benefits of meditation are largely cumulative. This means that you can't expect to meditate just once and discover the meaning of life. You need to meditate daily, preferably twice a day, and allow the benefits to come as gradually as they want to come. If you do this, then you will find that after several months, meditation becomes something that you simply cannot imagine living without.

OBEY THE GOLDEN RULE

The golden rule is a teaching central to almost all religious traditions, and can be expressed in any number of ways. Consider the following teachings from different religions:

- You shall love your neighbour as yourself. (Judaism and Christianity)

- Not one of you is a believer until he loves for his brother what he loves for himself. (Islam)

- A man should wander about treating all creatures as he himself would be treated. (Jainism)

143

- Try your best to treat others as you would wish to be treated yourself. (Confucianism)

- One should not behave towards others in a way that is disagreeable to oneself. (Hinduism)

No matter how the golden rule is stated, the principle is always the same. Treat others in the exact same way in which you would like to be treated. If you wouldn't like your partner to commit adultery, don't go sleeping around. If you wouldn't like your boss to cheat you, don't steal his equipment from the stationery supply cupboard. If you wouldn't like someone to cut you up on the motorway, don't cut up your fellow driver.

Of course, the golden rule formula works in the opposite direction too, in that it encourages you to do things that you **would** like others to do to you. Would you like people to smile more often? Then smile more often yourself. Do you think it would be great if people said 'please' and 'thank you' more often? Then make sure you always say 'please' and 'thank you'.

Applying the golden rule to our lives helps us to get the maximum possible benefit from another ancient spiritual truth: 'We reap what we sow', or in more modern terms, 'What goes around comes around'. It provides us with an instant code of ethics that ensures that we never do anything questionable, and it therefore enables us to become more spiritual individuals, aware of the role we play in our own fate.

I won't spend any more time discussing the theology of the golden rule. The fact is that you've heard this rule a thousand times already. You know what to do, so just apply it in your own life and reap the benefits.

Read scriptures

A scripture is basically any text that is deemed to be sacred because it contains inspirational and practical teaching on matters of the spirit. There are many different scriptures in the world, because there are many different spiritual paths. But the thread of truth – the truth that there is a 'divine spark' within each of us – is common to all. Because of this, you should feel free to study any and all scriptures that appeal to you.

Some people feel that reading a wide range of scriptures from different traditions and paths makes the sacred lose its sacredness, but this is not the case. There are many benefits to studying scriptures from a variety of traditions.

● You will discover that virtually all religions agree on central key points and ideas. They may present and explain these ideas in different ways, but the truths themselves, like the golden rule, are often identical.

● Studying a variety of scriptures gives you a wide, balanced view of the ways in that the spiritual nature of humanity has been understood and related to in the past.

● You will learn a great number of additional spiritual techniques and principles that you may then wish to adopt in your own life.

Your choice of scriptures that you study is up to you. You can study ancient scriptures such as the Bible, Koran or the Bhagavadgita, or you could study more modern spiritual texts such as *A Course in Miracles*. You may also examine texts that, though not officially scriptures, still have much to offer in the way of insight, such as *Science of Mind* by Ernest Holmes and *Practising the Presence* by Joel Goldsmith.

If you wish to develop your spiritual life as quickly and efficiently as possible, I recommend that you read the scripture(s) of your choice for no less than 15 minutes each day, preferably in the morning, either before or after your meditation. Start a journal so that you can note down any particular points that you would like to contemplate further, and as you study, allow your intuition to elaborate on what you read.

Experiencing spiritual fulfilment is not like achieving millionaire status or achieving a qualification in your career. The fact is that in your spiritual life you will never truly 'arrive' at a point where you can honestly state that you have learned all there is to learn. In truth, the more you develop your spiritual nature, the more you will realise how little you know, and this is just as it should be.

Spiritual fulfilment comes from growing, not from arriving. The more you grow, the more fulfilled you will feel, and the more perspective you will have when looking at other areas of your life.

Summary of Part 2

You now have all the information you need to achieve your goals in seven specific areas of your life. To summarise, here are the key points:

- To secure your long-term financial success, increase your income and control your expenditure, then put any surplus money to good use.

- To achieve your health and fitness goals, eliminate poisons from your system, adopt a healthy diet (aiming for an equal balance between proteins and carbohydrates and drinking plenty of water) and make regular exercise an integral part of your new lifestyle.

- Aim to go as far as you can in terms of career success by first making sure that you are in the right career. Then start viewing yourself as self-employed; do more than you are paid to do; always strive to improve your personal effectiveness and communication skills; and don't forget to have outside interests that are unrelated to your career.

- Improve your relationships by understanding and applying the generic, platonic and intimate rules that are detailed fully in Chapter 7.

- Take greater control of your emotions. Learn to understand and use music and the body/mind connection to influence your mood.

- To improve family relationships quite dramatically, set yourself just four goals: plan to spend time together regularly; create a harmonious home environment; improve your communication skills; and learn to be more tolerant and respectful of others.

- Transform the way you view yourself and the world around you by spending time on your spiritual life. Learn to meditate, obey the golden rule, which is common to all religions, and read a variety of inspirational and sacred texts. These things will all help to provide genuine peace of mind and a deep sense of meaning to your life.

Apply what you have learned by **being** and **doing** and you will **have** all that you want from life – and much more besides.

Conclusion

There are two types of people in the world: those who dream, and those who take action. Those who dream may enjoy elaborate fantasies of success and achievement, but will never get to experience these things in the real world. Those who take action, on the other hand, will experience both tangible and intangible successes in all areas of their lives.

So it isn't what you think or know that determines where you will be in five, ten or 20 years' time. It's what you do – today, tomorrow and every day that follows.

I sincerely hope that after reading this book you will decide to commit yourself to becoming one of life's doers, and not just an idle dreamer. Achieving success won't always necessarily be easy, but it can be simple and if you follow my advice, it will be. Just be the kind of person you need to be, do the things you need to do, and you will have all the success you want. And remember, the sooner you change your lifestyle, the sooner you will change your ultimate destiny.

So start right now!

Useful Resources

GENERAL SUCCESS AND ACHIEVEMENT

Books

Allen, James, *As a Man Thinketh*, Courage Books, 2001
McGraw, Dr Phillip C., *Life Strategies*, Vermilion, 2001
Ringer, Robert J., *Looking Out for No. 1*, Fawcett Books, 1983
Ringer, Robert J., *Million Dollar Habits*, Fawcett Books, 1991
Robbins, Anthony, *Awaken the Giant Within*, Pocket Books, 2001
Robbins, Anthony, *Unlimited Power*, Simon and Schuster, 1998

Web sites

www.anthonyrobbins.com
www.oprah.com
www.topachievement.com

FINANCIAL SUCCESS

Books

Bruce, Ian, *Understand Shares in a Day*, Take That, 2001
Chan, James, *Spare Room Tycoon*, Nicholas Brealey Publishing Ltd, 2000
Clason, George S., *The Richest Man in Babylon*, Signet Books, 2002
Cohen, Bernice, *The Armchair Investor*, Orion, 1999
Hall, Alvin, *Your Money or Your Life*, Hodder and Stoughton, 2002

Hill, Napoleon, *Think And Grow Rich*, Renaissance Books, 2001

Kiyosaki, Robert T., *Rich Dad, Poor Dad*, Time Warner Books, 2002

Orman, Suzie, *The Courage to Be Rich*, Riverhead Books, 2001

Wattles, Wallace D. *The Science of Getting Rich*, Iceni Books, 2002

Web sites

www.moneyweb.co.uk
www.pensionguide.gov.uk
www.scienceofgettingrich.net
www.ukcreditcardsguide.co.uk
www.uk-invest.com
www.ukloansguide.co.uk
www.uksharesguide.co.uk
www.ukmortgagesguide.co.uk

HEALTH AND FITNESS

Books

Eggar, Robin, *The Royal Marines Total Fitness*, Vermilion, 1993
Jameson, Judy, *Fat Burning Foods*, Foulsham, 1997
Phillips, Bill, *Body for Life*, HarperCollins, 2001
Reyneke, Dreas, *Ultimate Pilates*, Vermilion 2002
Roberts, Matt, *Fitness for Life Manual*, Dorling Kindersley, 2002
Scrivener, Jane, *Detox Yourself*, Piatkus Books, 1997

Web sites

www.bodyforlife.com
www.cyberdiet.com

www.fitnesslink.com
www.health-club.net
www.healthgate.com
www.mensfitness.com
www.nhsdirect.nhs.uk
www.phys.com

CAREER SUCCESS

Books

Fox, Jeffrey J., *How to Become CEO*, Vermilion, 2000
Johnson, Dr Spencer, *Who Moved My Cheese?*, Vermilion, 1999
Mackay, Harvey, *Pushing the Envelope*, Ballantine Books, 2000
Simpson, Liz, *Working from the Heart*, Vermilion, 1999
Canfield, Jack, Hansen, Mark Victor, and Hewitt, Les, *The Power Of Focus*, Vermilion, 2001
Ryan, Robin, *60 Seconds and You're Hired!*, Vermilion, 2001

Web sites

www.careersolutions.co.uk
www.peoplebank.com
www.jobsearch.co.uk

SUCCESSFUL RELATIONSHIPS

Books

Carnegie, Dale, *How to Win Friends and Influence People*, Hutchinson, 1994
Cox, Tracey, *Hot Sex*, Corgi, 1999
Gray, John, *Men Are from Mars, Women Are from Venus*, HarperCollins, 2002

Litvinoff, Sarah, *Better Relationships*, Vermilion, 2001
McGraw, Dr Phillip C., *Relationship Rescue*, Vermilion, 2000
Ornish, Dr Dean, *Love and Survival*, Vermilion, 2001
Renshaw, Ben, *The Secrets*, Vermilion, 2002
Stone, Carol, *Networking*, Vermilion, 2001

Web sites

www.philmcgraw.com
www.relationship-talk.com

EMOTIONAL SUCCESS

Books

Burns, Dr David, *Ten Days to Great Self-esteem*, Vermilion, 2000
Cleese, John, and Skynner, Robin, *Life and How to Survive It*, Arrow, 1994
D'Ambra, Gilles, *Measure Your EQ Factor*, Foulsham, 1999
Field, Lynda, *60 Ways to Feel Amazing*, Vermilion, 2000
Hare, Beverley, *Be Assertive*, Vermilion, 1996
Jeffers, Susan, *Feel the Fear and Do It Anyway*, Rider, 1997
O'Connor, Joseph, *NLP Workbook*, HarperCollins, 2001
Taylor, Ros, *Confidence in Just Seven Days*, Vermilion, 2001

Web sites

www.nlpcomprehensive.com
www.nlpresources.com

FAMILY SUCCESS

Books

Cleese, John, and Skynner, Robin, *Families and How to Survive Them*, Vermilion, 1993

Kashani, Javad H., *How to Raise a Happy Child*, Vermilion, 2000

Hartley-Brewer, Elizabeth, *Positive Parenting*, Vermilion, 1994

Web sites

www.parents-talk.com
www.relate.org.uk

SPIRITUAL FULFILMENT

Books

HH The Dalai Lama, *Ancient Wisdom, Modern World*, Abacus, 2001

Lama Surya Das, *Awakening to the Sacred*, Bantam, 2000

Dyer, Dr Wayne, *Real Magic*, HarperPrism, 1993

Dyer, Dr Wayne, *Your Sacred Self*, HarperCollins, 1996

Smith, Erica, and Wilks, Nicholas, *Meditation*, Vermilion, 2001

Walsh, Roger, *Essential Spirituality*, Wiley and Sons Inc., 2000

Web sites

www.beliefnet.com
www.buddhanet.net
www.sacred-texts.com

Index